WHO *Are* YOU *to* JUDGE?

WHO *Are* YOU *to* JUDGE?

*Learning to Distinguish
Between Truths, Half-Truths and Lies*

ERWIN W. LUTZER

MOODY PRESS
CHICAGO

All Scripture quotations, unless otherwise indicated, are taken from the *Holy
Bible, New International Version*®. NIV®. Copyright © 1973, 1978, 1984 by In-
ternational Bible Society. Used by permission of Zondervan Publishing House.
All rights reserved.

Scripture quotations marked NASB are taken from the *New American Standard
Bible*®, © Copyright The Lockman Foundation 1960, 1962, 1963, 1968, 1971,
1972, 1973, 1975, 1977, 1995. Used by permission.

Scripture quotations marked NKJV are taken from the *New King James Version*.
Copyright © 1982, 1992 by Thomas Nelson, Inc. Used by permission. All
rights reserved.

Scripture quotations marked NRSV are from the *New Revised Standard Version* of
the Bible, copyright 1946, 1952, and 1971 by the Division of Christian Education of the National Council of the Churches of Christ in the USA. Used by permission. All rights reserved.

Scripture quotations marked KJV are taken from the King James Version.

Library of Congress Cataloging-in-Publication Data

Lutzer, Erwin W.
    Who are you to judge? / Erwin W. Lutzer.
        p. cm.
    Includes bibliographical references.
    ISBN 0-8024-0943-1
    1. Christian ethics. I. Title.
BJ1251 .L88 2002
241--dc21

                                                             2002005273

13 5 7 9 10 8 6 4 2

Printed in the United States of America

For John Armstrong,
a mentor, a prayer partner,
but above all, a friend.

"I thank my God every time I remember you."
Philippians 1:3

CONTENTS

BEFORE
YOU BEGIN

There was a time when truth mattered.

In fact, at times truth mattered so much that love was in short supply. Read some of the writings of the Reformers and you will be convinced that all too often truth eclipsed charity and being right was always more important than being kind. I have often wondered what might have happened if John Knox had shown Mary, Queen of Scots a bit more courtesy and compassion during his dialogues with her. We can't know, of course, but maybe her heart would have softened to the Reformed faith and the bitter conflicts might have become more charitable. We can say the same about the heated debate between Luther and Zwingli; and the rancor between Calvin and Servetus, who was burned at the stake in Geneva. A little understanding would have sweetened these conflicts.

In our day, we have drifted to the opposite extreme. Love has replaced truth, and, as for unity, it is more important than any doctrine—including the gospel. Better to tolerate heresy, the argument goes, than to risk looking unloving to the world. Thus, under the banner of unity, almost any doctrinal deviation is tolerated, and breaches of morality are quickly forgiven.

We might not always like the attitude of the Reformers, but their example is a necessary antidote to our permissive attitudes and lifestyles. They would tell us that no one has ever made it to heaven simply because he was loving; if one wishes to get to heaven, truth is needed. They would also warn us that there is such a thing as unity based on error. Jesus demonstrated that a spirit of love is not incompatible with warnings about error and even the denunciation of false teachers.

But where do we draw the line? At what point do we have to say, "Enough is enough"? Certainly we do not want to divide over nonessentials; we do not want to treat other believers with a "holier than thou" attitude, as if we are the only ones who are right. But at the same time we must blow the trumpet; we must call the church to be distinct from the world. We must treasure and defend the truth, even when we have to risk being misunderstood or cause a break in personal fellowship.

This is a book about *discernment*, the ability to distinguish the false from the true, or better, the false from the half-true. Of course, I do not expect that all Christians will agree with me about the various issues treated in the pages that follow, but I would like to think that this book will open up some needed dialogue on these subjects. I would be most pleased if we would think together about how the religious and moral dimensions of our culture have affected the church and what should be done about it. This is the task to which we have been called.

For the most part, I have not named names in my discussion of those who have opted for personal hunches and so-called prophecies in exchange for sound doctrine. My intention has been to give the basic principles needed for evaluation. Evangelists, pastors, faith healers, and prophets come and go, but God's Word abides.

Join me on a journey. Let's explore together how we might properly redraw those lines that distinguish the church from the world. Let us lovingly take up the task of warning, rebuking, and instructing one another with the hope that we might reclaim precious ground that has been lost as we have been inundated by the spirit of the world.

The task is urgent. Let's ask for God's strength to do what needs to be done.

ERWIN LUTZER
MOODY CHURCH, 2002

1

WHY ARE WE AFRAID TO JUDGE?

THE FUTURE IS HERE

The church is to be in the world as a ship is in the ocean; but when the ocean seeps into the ship, the ship is in trouble. I fear that the evangelical ship is taking on water. The world is seeping into the church so rapidly that we might well wonder how long the vessel can stay afloat. The church, which is called to influence the world, finds herself influenced *by* the world.

If we as Christ's representatives can scarcely stay afloat, how can we expect to rescue a society that is sinking around us? We have bought into the world's values; into its entertainment, its morals, its attitudes. We have also bought into its tolerance, its insistence that we should never challenge the private beliefs of individuals, whether outside the church or within it. In the face of cultural pressures, we have found ourselves confused, hesitant to act, unable to give a loving but convincing witness to the world.

Of course, there are also many hopeful signs in our culture. There are churches and individuals that are making a great impact for the gospel, and for that we are thankful. But for the most part, we as Christians have settled down to a comfortable kind of Christianity that demands very little and therefore, in turn, makes very little difference in the wider culture.

> WE HAVE LOST THE ABILITY TO JUDGE THE WORLD BECAUSE WE HAVE LOST THE ABILITY TO JUDGE OURSELVES.

When the world takes a step in our direction, we embrace it without a twinge of conscience. But a church that has made its peace with the world is incapable of changing it.

Today there is a myth that the world is more tolerant than it used to be because it accepts "both points of view." If you were to stand on a street corner in the cities of America and ask, "What do you think of Jesus Christ?" you would probably get a favorable response. He would be described as a good teacher or as one who taught us about love. But we can be quite sure that the world speaks well of Him because they misunderstand who He is and why He came to earth.

Listen to His own words: "If the world hates you, keep in mind that it hated me first. If you belonged to the world, it would love you as its own. As it is, you do not belong to the world, but I have chosen you out of the world. That is why the world hates you" (John 15:18–19). By and large the world of today has a favorable opinion of Christ only because it misinterprets Him.

Remember this axiom: The better the world understands the purpose of Jesus' coming, the more it hates Him.
What the world values, Christ despises; what He loves, it
hates. Years ago, F. B. Meyer wrote, "Between such irrecon-
cilable opposites as the church and the world, there cannot
be but antagonism and strife. Each treasures and seeks what
the other rejects as worthless. Each is devoted to ends that
are inimical to the dearest interests of the other."[1] And yet,
just think, most Christians think it is possible to follow Jesus
without turning their backs on the world!

Generations ago, we heard sermons titled "Biblical Separation," that is, sermons about the belief that we must separate ourselves from that which displeases God and commit
ourselves to the values and convictions of Scripture. Many
of us were warned about such things as movies, alcohol, to-
bacco, and a small cluster of other sins. This kind of instruction had its limitations because godliness was often
defined in terms of the things we were not supposed to do.
But at least we were taught that some things were right and
others were wrong; there was an attempt, however imperfect, to distinguish the church from the world.

My generation claimed to be wiser than our parents. We
said that the list of "worldly sins" was man-made and that
we had to make our own decisions about these matters.
Older Christians, who knew their hearts better than we
knew our own, warned that if we began to tolerate worldli-
ness, however it was defined, we would trip a series of
dominoes and the day would come when the church would
be filled with "worldly believers."

That day is here.

Opinion polls show that the difference between the

church and the world is, in some ways, indistinguishable. The sins that are in the world are in the church: divorce, immorality, pornography, risqué entertainment, materialism, and apathy toward what others believe. Officially, we believe that without trusting Jesus as Savior people are lost; unofficially, we act as if what people believe and the way they behave really does not matter. No wonder our light has become a flicker and our salt has lost its savor.

Many believe that we have no right to judge anyone's lifestyle or beliefs. Our commitment to radical individualism and the privatization of faith has made us willing to "live and let live" without discussion, evaluation, or rebuke. We have lost the ability to judge the world because we have lost the ability to judge ourselves. We affirm certain beliefs and then act as if they don't matter.

No wonder the most oft-quoted verse from the Bible is not "For God so loved the world" (John 3:16) but, rather, "Do not judge, or you too will be judged" (Matthew 7:1). Even in evangelical circles we sometimes hear, "Who are you to judge?" The clear implication of the question is that we have no right to say, "This lifestyle is wrong," or, "This is heresy," or again, "This preacher is a false teacher." The one word that best describes our culture is *Whatever!!!*

How did we get here?

Why do we find it so difficult to say that some religious views are wrong? Or that some kinds of behavior are sinful? Why do we allow so much of Hollywood into our homes, pretending that we and our families are not influenced by the entertainment industry? Why do we allow false teachers and prophets to flourish without warning the people of God? Why are various forms of occultism practiced? These are just some questions we will be discussing in the chapters that follow.

Before we begin our journey, we must have a better understanding of how the prevailing ideas of our culture have influenced the church. We might find that we are more affected by the world than we realize. So before we turn to speak about our responsibility as members of the church, we have to take a few moments to understand the challenges we confront in the world around us.

> TRUTH HAS DISAPPEARED, AND FEW HAVE NOTICED.

We've all heard that we are living in a postmodern society, but what does that mean? And how does postmodernism impact the church? Every generation must fight its own battles; sometimes the pressure points of one generation are the same as those of a previous one, but often the issues are different. But each generation must confront the world, either to change it or to be changed by it.

Today our challenges are unique, for no generation has been influenced by technology as has ours. We are bombarded with television, the video revolution, and the Internet. Perhaps no generation has had as many opportunities as ours; nor has any had as many pitfalls. In the midst of great opportunity, we have, I fear, turned from much that is good toward much that is trivial and even irrational. In our day there has been a mega-shift in thinking; this generation perceives reality differently from the way past generations did. Yes, people in general don't view life the way they used to, and we Christians don't either.

So let's take a brief tour into what is called the postmodern mind so that we might better understand the challenges before us. Then let's ask ourselves how we have been influenced by the world and what can be done about it.

DESCENDING INTO DECADENCE

Truth has disappeared, and few have noticed. Before our eyes, the old thought forms are crumbling, and in their place we find new ways of seeing the world and our experience of it. Some of us grew up with assumptions that are being discarded, and in their place are new assumptions that stand in direct opposition to the Christian gospel. Perhaps it is not too strong to say that war has been declared on the past in favor of a brave new future.

We can't understand postmodernism unless we understand what modernism was (and is). Modernism was the belief that reason had the power to make sense out of the world; the human mind, it was thought, has the ability to interpret reality and discover overarching values. It was optimistic, believing in progress; there was the belief that science and history could lead us to various truths that would help us interpret reality. Modernism attacked religion, particularly Christianity, because it believed Christianity was filled with superstitions, but at least modernism believed that truth existed and it was not afraid to say so.

> TRUTH IS NOW DEFINED AS MY PERSONAL OPINION OF REALITY.

Enter postmodernism.

The contemporary notion is that reason has failed to make sense out of the world. Indeed, modernism, it is said, does not have the building blocks necessary to construct a system of truths that would be applicable to all cultures. So the old assumption that there is objective truth must be replaced with the notion that there really is no "truth"—if by truth we mean values applicable to all cultures and all times. Truth, if it exists at all, does not exist "out there" to be discovered but rather is simply my own personal response to the data that is presented to me. I do not discover truth; I am the *source* of truth.[2]

Whereas modernism attacked religion as being superstition, postmodernism accepts all religions and gives a high place to all kinds of superstitions. Spirituality of every sort is now accepted without any suggestion that one point of view might be wrong and another right. Since truth is now defined as my personal opinion of reality, it follows that we have any number of "truths"—about as many as there are individuals in the world.

Theoretically, then, postmodernism says that there is no independent standard of right or wrong, no independent standard of truth and error. Yet, because we are moral beings, not even postmodernists can discard all moral judgments. When postmoderns see something they don't like, they have new ways of describing what they see; they have invented notions that replace the concept of truth.

These new thought forms have changed the dialogue in our modern world. We had best understand our culture if we wish to challenge it.

Truth Is Replaced by Fairness

As mentioned, time was when people believed truth existed, even though they disagreed as to what it was. Today, a belief is evaluated not on the basis of whether it is true or false but by asking, "Is it *fair?*"

Think of what this means for those of us who believe the gospel. The idea that salvation comes through Christ alone certainly does not appear "fair," given the many different religions in the world. Thus our message is ruled unacceptable no matter how much evidence might be adduced for it. In fact, what we believe, we are told, is based on narrow prejudice. Christianity is just our bias.

The same approach is taken in evaluating morality. Postmodernists say that morality, if it exists at all, is an exercise in psychology. So if you and I were to say, "I believe this to be immoral," the modern mind hears us saying, "I have this prejudice." We've all heard gay rights organizations refer to those who believe in the traditional marriage as people who are bigoted. In other words, morality is not a matter of objectivity but narrow, personal bias.

Perhaps this illustration from baseball will help. Someone has said that a pre-modern umpire would have said, "There are balls and there are strikes and I call 'em *as they are.*" A modern umpire would have said, "There are balls and there are strikes and I call 'em *as I see them.*" But a postmodern umpire would say, "There are balls and there are strikes and they are *whatever I call 'em.*" So in matters of religion and morality, truth is whatever I say it is.

Our national icon is inoffensiveness. So if you think you have the "truth," courtesy demands that you keep your thoughts to yourself. As a good citizen, you should have the civility to keep quiet about your privately held convictions (your prejudices). Even freedom of speech should not extend to making moral judgments about other people's private behavior.

To put it differently, a new "right" has been found in the Constitution. No one should ever have to hear anything with which he disagrees! No one should ever have to hear anything that offends him. "Hate Crimes Legislation" is touted to be a defense of those groups that are supposedly unfairly singled out for bigotry and criminal activity. Whatever the merits of this legislation, we should be aware that the goal is to declare "offensive language" as a hate crime, thus silencing freedom of speech.

For example, in Canada where such legislation has passed, authorities have warned Dr. James Dobson's *Focus on the Family* and Dr. Jerry Falwell's *Old Time Gospel Hour* and Dr. Laura Schlessinger that they cannot broadcast unless they cut any portions dealing with homosexuality. The Canadian broadcasting board cites Canada's "hate crime law," which says it is illegal to speak of any group derogatorily. This means that pastors cannot read Bible verses on the air regarding homosexuality, or they endanger the licenses of stations that carry them.[3]

Some take the argument a step further and say it is not just the perpetrator of crimes who is guilty; anyone who is not in step with the homosexual agenda is also guilty. Recall that after the homosexual Matthew Shepherd was murdered, a wide net of blame was cast that included all those who spoke against gay marriages and special rights for homosexuals. Thus since "anti-gay" expressions contribute to the crime of others, the postmodern stance is that such biases should be held privately—if for no other reason than because they are highly offensive.

Inoffensiveness also has impacted the political sphere. You will recall that after the September 11 terrorist attacks some businesses would not allow their employees to keep an American flag on their desks, for fear that they were offending other workers who were not in support of the war in Afghanistan. S. D. Gade, in his book *When Tolerance Is No Virtue*, says that the objective of political correctness (essentially another term for postmodernism) is to avoid invading anyone's "attitudinal space."[4]

The result is that we can bear only good news, not bad. You can say that Jesus has changed your life, but what is inadmissible is saying that He is the only way to God. For one thing, such statements are unfair because they make Jesus superior to other religious leaders, and this offends the majority of the world's population. What is more, such statements cannot be objectively true but are only the reflections of one's private religious bias. End of discussion.

Not everything about politically correct thinking is wrong. We Christians have often been judgmental, intolerant, and self-righteous at all the wrong points. We have been guilty of racism, elitism, and doctrinal snobbishness. There are some Christians who could use a good dose of tolerance, especially when it comes to their relationship with other Christians. But notice this: We should be tolerant in these areas, not because not doing so offends people, but because it is the right thing to do. In other words, *our tolerance must be based on truth, just as much as our intolerance must be based on truth.* In the end, our judgments must come down to truth questions.[5]

The problem is that we are often intolerant where we should be more tolerant; and often we are tolerant where we should be intolerant. In a word, we are intimidated. I, for one, do not have all the answers in our confused world, but we must attempt to be true to what the Bible teaches and live according to the mandate our Lord left for us.

We've learned that for the modern mind, there is no court of appeal in the traditional sense. Truth is subjective, disconnected from argumentation and facts. There is "your truth" and "my truth" but no truth that we must both claim. So our criterion for judging religious beliefs and lifestyles is not truth but fairness.

Truth Is Replaced by Sensuality

If individual perceptions are king, it follows that human beings will gravitate from the rational to the sensual. When God created man, two matters became inherently sacred. One was the sanctity of human life; the second was the sanctity of intimate sexuality. Today we have attacks against both: We have a society rampant with violence on television and on our streets; we also are obsessed with eroticism that destroys the sacredness of marriage.[6]

Our film and media industries have desensitized us to violence. In one study, when children were shown people being shot on television, they accepted it without much ado. But when they saw puppies being shot to death, they were horrified, crying out in righteous anger, shock, and grief. They had been conditioned to accept the violence that kills humans and outraged only at the violence that kills animals.

By nature we are not driven by rationality but by our desires. Without the restraints of laws and religion, mankind always drifts toward his urges, his immediate sensations.

Eve, standing before the forbidden tree, was mesmerized by its hidden powers. "When the woman saw that the fruit of the tree was good for food and pleasing to the eye, and also desirable for gaining wisdom, she took some and ate it" (Genesis 3:6). Her perceptions were more present to her than the commands of God. What she saw, felt, and anticipated was more alluring than obedience.

Left to themselves, human beings behave according to what feels right rather than according to what their mind and conscience tells them is right. Given the disintegration of basic moral distinctions, tolerance for any and every deviancy is in vogue. I've heard people say, "I can't deny my own feelings; they are a part of who I am, so I have to do what feels best." Years ago we saw a bumper sticker that said, "If it feels good, do it." Today, we have bumper stickers that say, "If it feels good, it is *right*." As for guilt, if it exists at all, it is just a feeling that has to be unlearned.

Since the ego has replaced God, people feel free to do whatever is necessary to find pleasure, no matter who gets hurt, no matter what the consequences. Since there can be no moral judgments that are applicable to all people at all times, and since morality is nothing more than what "seems good to me," no wonder we often hear the mantra, "Who are you to judge?"

Ravi Zacharias asks, "How do we communicate the gospel to a generation that hears with its eyes and thinks with its feelings?"[7] That is an excellent question, but it is beyond the scope and intention of this book. I'm more interested in making sure that we have a gospel left to communicate rather than investigating the question of how it should be communicated.

Our challenges lie on many fronts.

Truth Is Replaced by Mysticism

Religion is out; spirituality is in. What this means is that people are "into spirituality" without having to believe any doctrines. Since we no longer have objective truth but only individual perceptions, it follows that it does not matter if these perceptions contradict one another. If what I experience is true for me, who are you to say otherwise?

Deepak Chopra unites religious mysticism with medicine and teaches that the basic substance of our bodies is not matter but energy and information. We must become aware of the flow of human energy centered in channels known as *chakras*.[8] Healing takes place when we correct the flow of human energy and any imbalances in it. This is done by passing the hands over the other person, but without making contact. No contact is needed because the *Prana*, or vital energy, extends a few inches above the skin.

Chopra believes that at the core we are love, truth, compassion, awareness, and spirit. He says, "I am perfect as I am!"[9] Our problem is that we do not believe this; if we did, we would be healthy, for we are the source of our own strength and healing. Evil is denied, and "truth" is whatever happens to work. Beyond this, people are encouraged to experiment with occult phenomena.

From time to time we read stories about the value of prayer in healing physical ailments. In one controlled study, it was shown that people who were prayed for recovered much faster than others; indeed, there were even some evidences of rather miraculous healings. Most important, the report said it did not matter who did the praying, nor the deity before whom the names were invoked.

Whereas modernism said all religions were wrong, this new information about prayer apparently proves the postmodern notion that all religions are right. So today we are told that all religious points of view, no matter how logically contradictory, are equally valid. The mind, it is believed, creates its own reality. Ideas are "true" simply because I think them; truth is what I perceive it to be.

Understandably, we as Christians have a challenge before us, for our commitment to Christ commands us to make judgments in this nonjudgmental world.

THE CHALLENGE BEFORE US

We can't blame postmodernism for the condition of the church, but there is no doubt that we have all been influenced by its tolerant mood. Many Christians feel no obligation to share their faith with others. They believe their own convictions are good for them, and it would be nice if others became Christians, but they do not see any urgency for others to hear the Christian message! Perhaps this explains that, according to pollster George Barna, only 8 percent of adults have evangelical beliefs compared to 12 percent a decade ago. He says, "The number has dropped by a third as Americans continue to reshape their theological views."[10]

Many Christians feel embarrassed about the fact that we believe in universal truth, specifically in the uniqueness of Christ and His death and resurrection as the only means by which we can be accepted by God. In an age when the greatest sin is offensiveness, and the greatest virtue is inoffensiveness, it is difficult to share a message that, at its core, is offensive to the mind of fallen man.

What is more, we feel intimidated, not only to judge the lostness of the world, but also to judge the condition of the church. We are embarrassed by arguments over doctrine and the pettiness that has often accompanied church splits. Repeatedly, we have heard how terrible it is that Protestantism has fragmented into an endless number of denominations and that these splits have been a scandal to the watching world. As a result, we are afraid that any judgments we make will only further these divisions and portray the church as at war with itself.

> WE THINK IT IS BETTER TO TOLERATE ERROR THAN TO LOOK UGLY DEFENDING THE TRUTH.

Others take the quest for unity a step further and believe that even the division between Protestantism and Catholicism should be healed. Not until all of Christendom becomes one in organization, one in vision, and one in doctrine will the world believe, or so we are told. Since the Protestant Reformation began over a disagreement in doctrine, some are telling us that doctrine must be minimized if unity is to be achieved.

So in a world where doctrine is seen as the enemy of unity, it seems reasonable that "petty doctrinal issues," as they are sometimes called, must be set aside for the benefit of the oneness that will impress the world. To draw a line in the sand and say, "Here we stand," is to further divide a fractured church. Unity at all costs.

No wonder we are afraid to make judgments! We are told that we should unite, not divide; we should show love rather than cleave to our personal biases. We are to concentrate on our own failings, not the failings of others. Let love "cover a multitude of sins" is the banner that captures the mood of our generation.

Given such an atmosphere, we can better understand why we often have uncritically accepted the world's values, its misguided tolerance, its entertainment, and its commitment to selfish individualism. We have preferred to be quiet, standing by and watching our culture drift, feeling helpless amid the swelling tide. In our timidity we have lost the credibility that is needed to be a compelling witness to the world.

Surely we must agree that discernment is in short supply. Schooled in the idea that we should "live and let live," we have allowed worldly thinking to flourish. While occultism grows in the evangelical church, few are willing to sound the alarm; fewer yet are willing to identify the false prophets that abound or to give good reasons why the God of Islam is different from the God of Christianity. Thus multitudes keep being misled with nary a word of warning. We think it is better to tolerate error than to look ugly defending the truth.

And yes, we must admit that the church has often looked ugly. There have been unnecessary doctrinal disputes; there have been personality conflicts, and the egos of the leaders have often been the basis of division, bickering, and needless conflicts. But the fact remains that we have the responsibility of making judgments. We are to represent Christ in an age that pays Him lip service but endears its heart to other lovers.

Perhaps no passage of Scripture has been used as often and as effectively to discourage any judging of doctrine or religious teachers than the prayer Jesus offered in John 17.

Since He prayed for unity, some people have understood His words to mean that unity must supersede truth. They have argued that since doctrine divides, it should be minimized for the greater good of reaching the world.

But did Christ intend us to understand that we are not to judge doctrine? Did He want us to understand that unity is more important than truth? Do we need to set our disagreements aside in favor of a "united" church to impress the world? And what should the world see when it looks at the church?

FULFILLING THE PRAYER OF JESUS

There will always be tension between doctrinal integrity and unity. Jesus emphasized both in His prayer, and our responsibility is to find the balance between the two. In John 17:11, He prayed that His followers would be united: "Holy Father, protect them by the power of your name—the name you gave me—so that they may be one as we are one." A second time He prayed for the kind of unity that should impact the world, "that all of them may be one, Father, just as you are in me and I am in you. May they also be in us so that the world may believe that you have sent me" (v. 21). The unity for which He prayed is so powerful that the world should take notice and believe on Him. This is a unity that should be visible, credible, and supernatural.

But let us notice the following.

First, we are explicitly told that He is praying for unity among His true followers only. They are described as the ones to whom Christ revealed the Father (v. 6); they are the ones who have obeyed His word (v. 6). His prayer is directed in behalf of those who understand His uniqueness. He prays for those who recognize that He is a prophet, yes, but more than a prophet. His prayer is for those who believe in His name for their salvation and life's passion.

"I am not praying for the world," He says, "but for those you have given me, for they are yours" (v. 9). He does not pray for Judas, for he was not a gift from the Father to the Son; at no time did Judas belong to Him (v. 12). He prays only for His followers, that the powerful evil forces they would encounter would not disrupt their unity.

> THE LOVE WITHIN THE CHURCH *ATTRACTS* THE WORLD; THE HOLINESS WITHIN THE CHURCH *CONVICTS* THE WORLD.

This most assuredly is not a prayer in behalf of worldwide Christendom as such; it is not a prayer for the visible, organizational unity of the church, regardless of her beliefs and teachings. Whatever we may say about contemporary Roman Catholicism, the fact is that during the days of the Reformation, the church had veered far from the teachings of the Bible, particularly in matters of salvation. To say that the Reformers should have maintained organizational unity even in the face of serious doctrinal error is certainly to miss Jesus' point. Unity among believers, yes; unity with those who teach a false gospel, no.

Jesus' prayer began to be answered when the Holy Spirit came at Pentecost and united all believers into the body of Christ. This prayer continues to be answered when new believers are granted the gift of the Holy Spirit and are baptized into the same body (1 Corinthians 12:13). This prayer transcends all denominations and groups; it is a prayer that transcends all races, cultures, and genders. It is a prayer for all who have been truly born of the Spirit in every country and corner on earth.

Second, Jesus prayed that this unity would be a unity supported by truth. "Sanctify them by the truth; your word is truth" (v. 17). Here He prays for the purity of the church; He prays that His believers would be set apart for the Father's blessing and use. He is asking that the church would be pure, separate from the world, and committed to her mission. "As you sent me into the world, I have sent them into the world" (v. 18).

What is the world to see when it looks at the church?

The world should be attracted by our observable unity, based on truth. Just hours before this prayer, Jesus told His disciples, "By this all men will know that you are my disciples, if you love one another" (John 13:35). Since this love is to be seen, it is my opinion that Jesus was thinking primarily of the love that exists within members of a given congregation, not necessarily the broad organizational unity that many think is the key to winning the world.

Please don't misunderstand. I'm not saying that outward unity is optional because we already have the unity of the Spirit. There is little doubt that we should strive "to keep the unity of the Spirit through the bond of peace," as Paul urges us to do (Ephesians 4:3). The history of the church is filled with many examples of needless division, either based on personalities or trivialities. The fragmentation of Protestantism has, at times, been a scandal that no doubt has made the world turn away in disgust. *But we cannot fulfill the prayer of Jesus by sacrificing our differences, especially when those differences lie at the heart of the gospel.*

What is more, it is doubtful that the world would rush to believe if only all the Protestant denominations dropped their labels or if giant rallies were held in a stadium, proving that we have now all become "one." Nor, in my opinion, would the union of Protestantism and Catholicism cause a wave of conversions. Such a unity might initially bring headlines, but its effects would eventually dissipate.

People will be impressed when we become a community of caring people whose sacrifice for others cannot go unnoticed. Our fractured homes have produced a sense of betrayal and worthlessness that only deep friendships can begin to heal. Individual believers living the life of Christ shoulder to shoulder with the skeptical people of the world will give credibility to our message. We must be committed to helping the poor, standing with the oppressed, and expending ourselves for those who have dismissed Christianity as irrelevant.

Intellectual arguments alone will not win a generation schooled in the notion that worldviews should not be judged by rational consistency or evidence. Christianity, rooted in the soil of history and reason, finds it difficult to compete in an age given to irrational commitments. But a life committed to the betterment of others is difficult to refute. As Francis Schaeffer used to tell us, the local church "should not only be right, but beautiful." Love will win them.

Third, Jesus prayed for the *holiness* of the church. "My prayer is not that you take them out of the world but that you protect them from the evil one. They are not of the world, even as I am not of it. Sanctify them by the truth; your word is truth" (John 17:15–17).

The church is to be "sanctified," that is, to be a community of believers who embrace integrity, purity, and a passionate love for God. The values of the world are to be rejected; indeed, the Bible says of the one who loves the world, "the love of the Father is not in him" (1 John 2:15).

Mark this well: The love within the church *attracts* the world; the holiness within the church *convicts* the world. In the early church, great fear came upon the people when they saw the church committed to discipline and holy living. Unfortunately, as the world observes the church today it might see a commitment to love (which it views as tolerance), but I doubt that it sees a commitment to holy living. Yet we are called to both.

> THE CHURCH DESPERATELY NEEDS CREDIBILITY AT THIS MOMENT OF HISTORY.

We are, says Peter, a chosen people, "a royal priesthood, a holy nation, a people belonging to God, that [we] may *declare the praises of him* who called [us] out of darkness into his wonderful light" (1 Peter 2:9; emphasis added). I agree with Dwight Edwards, who says, "As today's unbelievers observe God's children living in radical holiness, in supernatural community, and in overflowing grace, they too will be provoked to consider Christ in ways that a thousand tracts could never do."[11]

If the call to holiness is to be obeyed, we must have discernment. To be set apart for God means that we identify the world's values and that we choose to live to the beat of a different drummer. To be in the world but not of it is the challenge before us.

How can we represent Christ effectively in an age of religious superstitions and radical individualism? How can we maintain that critical balance between holiness and unity?

The sanctification for which Jesus prayed demands that we recommit ourselves to those truths that have made the church great.

THE PURPOSE OF THIS BOOK

The purpose of this book is to redraw some blurred lines between the church and the world. It is to ask ourselves what Jesus meant when He said that we should be "in the world, but not of it." We must understand the world *from* which we have been called, and we must also understand the holy calling *to* which we have been called.

In the pages that follow, I intend to shed some light on the neglected topic of discernment, that is, the ability to distinguish biblical Christianity from the counterfeit spirituality and values of today's world. My goal is to help all of us become vigilant, high-impact Christians who love truth and are willing to live by it even at great personal cost.

I believe that the church desperately needs credibility at this moment of history. I agree with S. D. Gade, who says that the most important question we face is, "What does it mean to be people of truth and justice at an hour such as this?"[12] Do we care? Or do we feel safe in our cocoon, walled off from a crumbling society? How can we be the church at this critical moment of history?

We must lovingly speak truth to this generation. We must not think that the task is impossible, for God by the Spirit works to convict men and women of the truth. We have help on our side. We have to model discernment and jealously guard the truth for the benefit of our children and grandchildren. Only a torch that is lit will ignite the next generation.

Of course we must be careful. We must choose our battles and season our judgments with love. When some people "think they smell heresy," John Stott says, "their nose begins to twitch, their muscles ripple, and the light of battle enters their eye. They seem to enjoy nothing more than a fight."[13] Others make the opposite mistake and believe that love requires them to overlook gross error.

Stott continues, "Truth becomes hard if it is not softened by love; love becomes soft if it is not strengthened by truth."[14] The balance is difficult, but we have no option but to attempt it. We must get the water out of the ship if we hope to rescue those who are drowning.

You might disagree with my judgments, but I hope you do agree that judgments are both necessary and needed. Let's try to find out what Jesus meant when He said, "Do not judge or you too will be judged" (Matthew 7:1).

Our task is to make wise judgments in a nonjudgmental world.

NOTES

1. F. B. Meyer, *Love to the Uttermost: Expositions of John 13–21* (New York: Revell, 1899), 135.

2. Jim Leffel and Dennis McCallum, "Postmodern Impact: Religion," in Dennis McCallum, ed., *The Death of Truth* (Minneapolis: Bethany House, 1996), 211.

3. *Family Voice,* July/August, 2001, 23.

4. S. D. Gade, *When Tolerance Is No Virtue* (Downers Grove, Ill.: InterVarsity, 1993), 22.

5. Ibid., 28–29.

6. Ravi Zacharias, "An Ancient Message, through Modern Means, to a Postmodern Mind," in D. A. Carson, ed., *Telling the Truth: Evangelizing Postmoderns* (Grand Rapids: Zondervan, 2000), 24.

7. Ibid., 26.

8. Dónal P. O'Mathúna, in "Postmodern Impact: Health Care," in *The Death of Truth,* 60.

9. Ibid., 72.

10. George Barna, "Religious Beliefs Vary Widely by Denomination," Barna Research Online, 25 June 2001, www.barna.org/cgi-bin.

11. Dwight Edwards, *Revolution Within* (Colorado Springs: Waterbrook, 2001), 24–25.

12. S. D. Gade, *When Tolerance Is No Virtue,* 17.

13. John Stott, *God's New Society: The Message of Ephesians* (Downer's Grove: InterVarsity, 1979), 172.

14. Ibid.

2

JUDGE NOT, THAT YOU BE NOT JUDGED

Should We Stop Making Judgments?

S o, who are *you* to judge?"

That was the question asked by a participant in a Bible study, after the teacher said that those who slept together before marriage were displeasing God.

"And, by the way, who of us is perfect?" the student continued. "We have no right to sit in judgment of someone else's personal morality."

So, who are *you* to judge?

We hear it every day:

- Who are you to say that God can't approve of loving homosexual relationships?
- Who are you to say that the Jehovah's Witnesses are wrong?

- Who are you to say that when people collapse because they are "slain in the spirit" by an anointed preacher— who are you to say they are not being "slain" by the Holy Spirit?
- Who are you to say that if someone is healed in a meeting, this might not be done by the power of God? And who are you to say that when a statue of the Virgin Mary weeps we should not think that she is trying to get a message to us?

Bring up the subject of judging and you will get two different responses. First, there are those who are unwilling to make any significant judgments; they are determined to "live and let live," within reason, of course. Short of criminal activity, they believe that everyone should be able to choose his own values and lifestyle, and neither the church nor individual Christians have a right to "judge" them.

But there are others who are all too willing to judge; they love to sharpen their arrows, identify their target, and let those around them know what God really thinks. Unfortunately, these are often critical people who not only judge others with the wrong attitude but for the wrong reasons. Often they judge others, not because of some actual breach of biblical conduct or doctrine but because of petty taboos or minor infractions. Often these critics are angry and resentful of those who do not measure up to their privately held convictions. Like the Pharisees, some see only the letter of the law and neglect the more important matters of justice, mercy, and love.

I believe that Jesus was speaking to both groups when He said, "Do not judge, or you too will be judged. For in the same way you judge others, you will be judged, and with the measure you use, it will be measured to you" (Matthew 7:1–2). But what did He mean by these words? Did He mean that we do ourselves a favor if we make no judgments, since such judgments will return upon our own heads? I think not.

We can be sure that Jesus was not teaching that we should not make judgments! To say, as some do, that we should take Jesus at face value and foster a mood of unity and appeasement; to say that we should have a tolerant attitude that never expresses opinions about what others believe and do—such are not the teachings of Christ. The argument that unity is more important than truth, and love more important than right doctrine, is wrong to the core.

Just consider the immediate context of Jesus' words. "Do not give dogs what is sacred; do not throw your pearls to pigs. If you do, they may trample them under their feet, and then turn and tear you to pieces" (v. 6). How could we possibly obey these instructions unless we learned to recognize dogs and pigs? Jesus was making a powerful statement about the need for discrimination, for learning to distinguish between what is clean and unclean, evaluating what is wise and what is foolish. All of this presupposes that we should make good judgments.

Next, look at the more remote context: "Watch out for false prophets. They come to you in sheep's clothing, but inwardly they are ferocious wolves" (v. 15). How can we beware of false prophets unless we can identify them? We are supposed to be looking for certain distinguishing marks of false teachers so that we can avoid them and warn others (an entire chapter of this book will be devoted to this).

Only a few verses later, Jesus made an even more startling remark, "Not everyone who says to me, 'Lord, Lord,' will

HOW CAN WE BE
GUARDED FROM
PHARISAISM ON THE
ONE HAND AND
MINDLESS GULLIBILITY
ON THE OTHER?

enter the kingdom of heaven, but only he who does the will of my Father who is in heaven. Many will say to me on that day, 'Lord, Lord, did we not prophesy in your name, and in your name drive out demons and perform many miracles?' Then I will tell them plainly, 'I never knew you. Away from me, you evildoers!'" (vv. 21–23). Here we have a powerful statement about the presence of false prophets, who are apparently able to do wonderful miracles but will be turned away from heaven's gate in the Day of Judgment. We can be wrong about many things, but let us not be wrong about false teachers and their doctrines!

Paul, the writer of many books in the New Testament, agreed with Jesus about the need for making judgments. When the believers in Corinth failed to excommunicate an immoral man from their assembly, Paul said that he himself had passed judgment on the transgressor, and that the church had better put him out of the congregation, so that his "spirit [might be] saved on the day of the Lord" (1 Corinthians 5:4). How could the church possibly exercise such authority unless its leadership made judgments?

In the very next chapter, Paul taught that believers should not take other believers to court in the presence of worldly judges because the leaders of the church itself should handle such disputes. He wrote, "Do you not know that the saints will judge the world? And if you are to judge the world, are you not competent to judge trivial cases? Do you not know that we will judge angels? How much more the things of this life!" (1 Corinthians 6:2–4). He went on to say that they should be ashamed that they were unable to make wise judgments about such matters.

Seems almost every week I hear another story of Christians filing lawsuits against other Christians. As our culture grows more litigious, so does the church. Just recently I heard that a Christian denomination filed a lawsuit against a Christian man whom they deemed owed them money. They did not even write to him first, trying to resolve the matter. In an unrelated case, a one-time supposed Christian leader filed suit against a church, justifying the suit by saying that he had retained a Christian attorney who had "found a way to get around the teaching of Scripture."

Imagine finding a way to "get around" the teaching of the Bible! Unfortunately, in many instances, Christians do not even attempt to "get around" God's Word; they simply ignore it. According to a recent Barna survey, "only four out of every ten born again adults rely upon the Bible or church teachings as their primary source of moral guidance."[1] If ever we needed instruction on judging, it is today!

What, then, did Jesus mean when He said, "Do not judge, or you too will be judged" (Matthew 7:1)? To put it briefly, He was teaching that we should not make Pharisaical judgments. We are not to be Pharisees, who loved to judge and therefore judged the wrong things; or even if they did make right judgments, made them for the wrong reasons. They exhibited a "holier than thou" tone in everything they did and said. We could say that Jesus is warning us, "Don't become a Pharisee, but *do* make righteous judgments."

How can we be guarded from Pharisaism on the one hand and mindless gullibility on the other? How do we know what should be judged and how judgments are to be made? What are the parameters to guide us? These are questions that must be addressed. Keep in mind that the word *judge* means to exercise discernment; at other times it can mean to condemn; and sometimes both ideas are present. But clearly Jesus is not teaching that all judging is wrong. Judging, or discernment, lies at the heart of Christian living.

PRINCIPLES OF BIBLICAL JUDGMENTS

Not a one of us makes perfect judgments. Even godly people often disagree regarding the relative merits of some matters or the way judgments should be handled. But if we can agree on the following principles, we have a basis for judging. Here are some guidelines that should help us make discerning judgments.

Humility, Not Superiority

We've already learned that the Pharisees were too anxious to judge. They had a critical spirit and wanted to believe the worst about others. Sadly, we must report that they were pleased when they found the faults they were looking for. Like the elder brother in the story of the Prodigal Son, the self-righteous person resents God's grace in the lives of great sinners. He cannot rejoice over the blessings the Father has poured out upon people he believes deserve punishment. The Pharisee wants to make sure that everyone follows his prescribed rules, even if he himself does not do so in private. If not, he wants them severely judged.

Let's consider Jesus' humorous illustration, "Why do you look at the speck of sawdust in your brother's eye and pay no attention to the plank in your own eye? How can you say to your brother, 'Let me take the speck out of your eye,' when all the time there is a plank in your own eye?" (7:3–4). As a metaphor, the eye represents the soul, that part of us that "sees," spiritually speaking; it refers to that part of us that reasons, thinks, and wills. Just a few verses earlier, Jesus said,

> SIN ALWAYS DISTORTS OUR PERCEPTIONS.

"The eye is the lamp of the body. If your eyes are good, your whole body will be full of light. But if your eyes are bad, your whole body will be full of darkness. If then the light within you is darkness, how great is that darkness!" (6:22–23). Obviously, it is important that we have a clear eye, that is, a mind and heart free of impurities.

You and I have met the kind of person Jesus describes as having a "plank" in his eye. He is usually a church member who claims that he is interested in truth; he tells you he is concerned about the health of the body of Christ. So he is anxious to remove the piece of sawdust from your eye and also the eyes of others. But the better you get to know him you realize that he is not interested in truth after all. If he were, he would take the plank out of his own eye first!

Obviously, Jesus intended that we see the humor in it all: Visualize a man with a plank in his eye walking through the lobby of the church trying to find a person with a speck of sawdust in his eye that he might remove it! The very image of such a man looking into a mirror but unable to see the plank in his eye because he is blinded by the plank is funny indeed.

Now, of course, if the man were thoroughly honest, if he were motivated by a sincere desire to please the Lord, then he would be as particular about himself as he is about others. He would go through great pains to remove the plank from his own eye first and then begin to look for others he might help. As D. Martyn Lloyd-Jones put it, "If a man claims that his only interest is in righteousness and truth, and not at all in personalities, then he will be as critical of himself as he is of other people."[2]

Here's a basic principle of human nature: People often see the sawdust in another's eye as a plank; and they see their own plank as a small speck of sawdust! I can recall a critical, mean, and angry woman who complained about a lack of love in the church! Denying the ugly part of herself, she was free to be very judgmental of others. Similarly, grace did not humble the Pharisees, for they minimized their own sins but magnified the sins of others.

Some people live in two worlds. In world A, they might be Sunday school teachers, elders, and trusted Christian leaders. But in world B, they might be committing adultery, nursing an addiction, or being just plain self-driven. Sometimes they find fault with others, hoping that their own reputation will be enhanced by comparison. Such a man sees the sawdust in others precisely because he is trying to prove that he can "see," despite the plank that is in his own eye. He believes his plank is so well hidden that no one can see it—and that the fact that he can "see" sawdust in someone else's eye proves it!

An engaged couple came to me because the man was

unable to forgive his girlfriend, who had confessed to a series of sexual relationships years before her conversion. Despite the engagement, he did not think he could marry someone who was not a virgin; he wanted someone who was pure, without the memories of other intimacies.

So I asked him whether he was a sexual "virgin." No, turns out that he also had a series of sexual relationships in college. When I asked him about this double standard, he admitted that, yes, it didn't make sense, but facts are facts: He simply could not forgive her. I pointed out that his problem was that he would not allow his past sin to humble him; yes, he had sinned, but his sin was different. His plank had grown so large that he couldn't "see" it! *You will never understand the heart of a Pharisee unless you realize that he sees the plank in his eye as belonging to others.*

> TAKING THE BEAM OUT OF OUR OWN EYE SHOULD BE OUR FIRST PRIORITY.

Sin always distorts our perceptions. When Nathan confronted David with a story about a rich man who had stolen a poor man's lamb, David was livid with anger and said, "As surely as the LORD lives, the man who did this deserves to die! He must pay for that lamb four times over, because he did such a thing and had no pity" (2 Samuel 12:5–6). Then Nathan said to David, "You are the man!" (v. 7). David could see how evil it was to steal a man's lamb, but he could not see the greater sin of stealing a man's wife and then murdering him to cover it up. Though blind to his own sins, he saw the sins of others with clarity.

Eye surgery is most delicate; a blind ophthalmologist cannot possibly remove the speck out of another person's eye. Christ's point: We have no right to judge others until we have been willing to admit the truth about ourselves. Perhaps one of the greatest problems in our churches is that we do not mourn over our own personal sin. We sin without brokenness, without a full recognition of our wrongs in God's presence. We think our sin is superficial, so we deal with it superficially.

When we have the courage to see ourselves in God's presence, we will never judge others in a wrong way. Having taken the plank out of our own eye, we will now see clearly to remove the speck from our brother's eye. Paul wrote, "Brothers, if someone is caught in a sin, you who are spiritual should restore him gently. But watch yourself, or you also may be tempted" (Galatians 6:1).

The more humble we are, the more mercy we will show to others. Those who have been given mercy should exercise mercy; those who have stood in great need of grace should invite others to accept great grace.

Facts, Not Presumptions

If we are quick to judge, we will not need much evidence to form our judgments. Fragments of information will be sufficient for those who have already made up their minds about the conduct and beliefs of others. Some people think they have the right to "connect the dots" and draw conclusions based on their own intuitions, hunches, and prior desires. If they are angry or savor a critical spirit, they will be likely to jump to conclusions. No wonder we read, "He who answers before listening—that is his folly and his shame" (Proverbs 18:13).

I remember forming a negative judgment about someone based on an E-mail I received. I did not know that the sender had his own skewed perspective; indeed, turns out he had a plank in his own eye. No matter how long I live, I still marvel at how skewed a perspective can be when you hear only one side of the story. The context, the reasons, the motivations—all of these enter into making proper judgments.

As human beings, we are always limited in our knowledge. It is impossible for us to know everything about anything; thus we admit that our judgments might be wrong. But we must try to safeguard against hasty judgments by doing research, asking questions, and having proper witnesses. There was a reason Paul wrote to Timothy, "Do not entertain an accusation against an elder unless it is brought by two or three witnesses" (1 Timothy 5:19).

Of course, today, the teachings of at least some false teachers are widespread, in books, television programs, and large rallies. Just so, the conduct of some Christians has come to light, as one revelation after another rocks the Christian world. And yet, we cannot be too careful; we dare not be hasty, but ask God to help us make wise judgments.

We must learn that sometimes we must withhold judgments. We cannot pronounce a verdict on every preacher, every movement, and every book or movie. Where we lack information, we must be cautious. Facts, not presumptions, must guide us.

Words and Actions, Not Motives

Only God knows the motives of the heart. I might see a TV preacher urge people to send him money and might be tempted to think that he is greedy, but maybe I do not know him well enough to make such a judgment. What I might be able to say, however, is that he is following in the path of the false prophets who have gravitated toward an emphasis on money (2 Peter 2:3). We are commanded to critique a man's (or a woman's) doctrine, methods, and lifestyle. But we are not qualified to judge the secrets of his soul.

A friend of mine, John Armstrong, reminded me that Satan made a mistake in judging the motives of Job. "Does Job fear God for nothing? . . . Have you not put a hedge around him and his household and everything he has? . . . But stretch out your hand and strike everything he has, and he will surely curse you to your face" (Job 1:9–11). Satan said that Job served God because of what he could get in return. But the devil was wrong about Job's motives; Job continued to serve God when everything was taken away from him. The devil erred when judging motives, and so do we.

Paul said that the opinions of others were of little concern to him:

> I care very little if I am judged by you or by any human court; indeed, I do not even judge myself. . . . Therefore judge nothing before the appointed time; wait till the Lord comes. He will bring to light what is hidden in darkness and will expose the motives of men's hearts. At that time each will receive his praise from God. (1 Corinthians 4:3, 5)

We are commanded to judge teachings and conduct; we are commanded to judge sinful behavior and attitudes; but motives belong to God and are beyond the realm of our knowledge and jurisdiction.

The fact that we can't know the motives of others should not stop us from assessing our own motives. We should ask: "Why are we concerned about making judgments? What are our motives for critiquing false teachers, entertainment, and the lifestyles of others and ourselves? Why read a book about judging?"

First, our motive should be to keep ourselves from error. Recalling the words of Jesus about the speck of sawdust and the plank, we must remember that taking the plank out of our own eye should be our first priority. We are anxious to know truth because we are anxious to be holy; we desire to please God, and so we want to know His mind regarding what we should believe and how we should live.

> WE HAVE NO RIGHT TO JUDGE OTHERS IN MATTERS OF CONSCIENCE WHERE THERE IS LATITUDE OF CONDUCT OR BELIEF.

Prudence also demands that we make sure that a ministry that claims it is using our money to help build an orphanage in Zambia is not actually using the funds to pay off the debt of a new headquarters building. All judging begins with the keen recognition that we are accountable to God for all of our talents and treasures and, particularly, our lifestyles and values. We want to be "as wise as serpents and as harmless as doves" because we ourselves will be evaluated by our Lord.

Second, our motive should be to guide others, to make sure that they are led in the path of salvation. Elders have a special responsibility toward the flock, Paul told the Ephesian elders:

"Keep watch over yourselves and all the flock of which the Holy Spirit has made you overseers. Be shepherds of the church of God, which he bought with his own blood. I know that after I leave, savage wolves will come in among you and will not spare the flock. Even from your own number men will arise and distort the truth in order to draw away disciples after them. So be on your guard! Remember that for three years I never stopped warning each of you night and day with tears." (Acts 20:28–31)

Later in this book, I will argue that the church of today has false teachers of various sorts. Television has given some men and women wide exposure, and many of them have millions of followers. Some of these teachers are spreading heresies that ultimately will destroy the faith of many. If you doubt this, spend some time reading Jude and 2 Peter, which are filled with warnings about the effects of false doctrine.

So, although we cannot judge the motives of others, let us ask God to judge our own inner motives. Let us make sure that we always judge with grace and mercy; let us not delight to find others in error. Every situation and person should be treated differently. "Be merciful to those who doubt; snatch others from the fire and save them; to others show mercy, mixed with fear—hating even the clothing stained by corrupted flesh" (Jude 22–23).

Let us try to limit our judgments to the words and actions of others and not impugn their motives.

Biblical Issues, Not Preferences

Some things are always right. We should always love one another; we should always abhor that which is evil; we should always do good to all men. On the other hand, some things are always wrong; it is always wrong to hate; it is always wrong to love evil or commit adultery. But there are some things that fall in between these two clearly defined spheres. Some matters become good or evil depending on the context, our motives, and who is affected by what we do.

When the controversy over eating meat was dividing the Christian community, Paul gave some important principles to help maintain reconciliation. He wrote that some Christians may eat meat, others only vegetables, but that both groups should accept each other. He wrote, "Accept him whose faith is weak, *without passing judgment on disputable matters*" (Romans 14:1, emphasis added). Then he added, "Who are you to judge someone else's servant? To his own master he stands or falls" (v. 4).

The point: We have no right to judge others in matters of conscience where there is latitude of conduct or belief. Some things might not be permissible for me but might be permissible for you, and vice versa. Perhaps one Christian has the freedom to drink wine, whereas it would violate the conscience of another. Then, again, even a Christian who has freedom might choose to not exercise it because it is a stumbling block to another (a later chapter in this book is devoted to this topic).

When we judge, we should be able to point to a verse of Scripture or a scriptural principle that undergirds our opinions. Ultimately, we are concerned about what God has revealed, not about our preferences and personal convictions. That means that we will not always agree with other Christians as to where the lines should be drawn. Sometimes we will find it almost impossible to separate ourselves from our culture, background, or temperament. And even if we could manage such a feat, we would still find that as humans we will experience areas of disagreement.

But let this not deter us from making necessary biblical judgments in a day when discernment is vilified as the enemy of love. We might not agree on the details, but the Bible is certainly clear enough to help us stay within divinely ordered parameters. Nor should we back away from discernment, even though we know that only God knows all the facts.

When we make judgments we must ask: What biblical truth is being denied? What truth is being substituted? What truth is being ignored? What truth is out of balance?

Temporal, Not Eternal Judgments

We've learned that the Pharisees not only judged the wrong things but acted as though they had the right to make final judgments. But such a prerogative belongs only to God. We have the power to judge, but we do not have the power to condemn; we have the right to warn but not the right to damn.

Let us return to the words of Jesus. He said, "Do not judge, or you too will be judged. For in the same way you judge others, you will be judged, and with the measure you use, it will be measured to you" (Matthew 7:1–2). What is the connection between our judgments and how we in turn will be judged? Jesus said that the measure we use for others will be the one used to measure us.

This phrase can be interpreted in two ways. It can mean that if you judge others they will judge you by your own yardstick. In other words, you will be treated as you treat others. There is some truth to this, for we all know that a harsh, judgmental person is usually judged more harshly by others. When the judgmental person trips up, we want to make sure that he gets "what is coming to him." One man, who was unusually strict and condemning when a fellow brother fell into immorality, discovered that he, in turn, received little mercy when he committed the same sin. Treat such people as they treat others, and they will cry foul, or worse.

Yet Jesus might have had another meaning in mind. Many commentators believe He meant that if you judge others with a strict standard you will be judged more strictly by God. We have examples of such judgments in the New Testament. Paul warned those who were irreverent when participating in Communion that they should judge themselves in this matter, so that they would not be "condemned with the world" (1 Corinthians 11:32). Some, who did not judge themselves, died under the hand of God's discipline.

Or consider these words, "You, therefore, have no excuse, you who pass judgment on someone else, for at whatever point you judge the other, you are condemning yourself, because you who pass judgment do the same things" (Romans 2:1). Such people are proving by their own judgments that they know what is right; but because they are no better, they condemn themselves. D. Martyn Lloyd-Jones asks, "Do I claim to have exceptional knowledge of Scripture? If I do, then I shall be judged in terms of the knowledge I claim. Do I claim that I am a servant who really knows these things? Then I should not be surprised if I am beaten with many stripes."[3] He adds, "If we sit as an authority in judgment upon others, we have no right to complain if we are judged by that very standard. It is quite fair, it is quite just, and we have no ground whatsoever for complaint."[4]

The Pharisees judged people by external matters, and they thought they had the right to condemn others in a final judgment. And what was worse, they judged others for things that they themselves were doing. Those who are quick to judge will be judged more strictly by God!

THE BOTTOM LINE

No wonder the subject of judging is fraught with challenges. On the one hand are the judgmental folks, quick to condemn and short on mercy; on the other hand are the "live and let live folks," who act as if nothing much matters to God.

Not all people with planks in their eyes are looking for sawdust in the eyes of others. Some who tolerate their own "planks" are all too happy to tolerate the "sawdust" and "planks" in the eyes of others. To be consistent, they judge neither themselves nor others.

One minister—bless him—preached a series of messages on the general theme that we should not judge others for their failures and sins. "Christians shoot their wounded," he said, and we must begin to understand that we all have our shortcomings; we would be better advised if we emphasized grace instead of judgment, love instead of criticism. In effect, he was touting the popular mantra, "Who are you to judge?"

Turns out he was having a long-standing adulterous affair during the weeks he was preaching the series of messages. He reasoned that he was more likely to get by with his sin if he looked the other way when he saw the sin of others. In effect what he was saying was: "My plank looks smaller in a room filled with people who all have planks of various shapes and sizes."

The ability to make judgments lies at the heart of Christian living. Unless we are able to judge doctrine, lifestyles, and entertainment; unless we are able to distinguish between outer appearances and inner character, we just might miss the purpose for which God placed us on this earth. We might end up accepting a stone for bread and a snake for a fish.

We do not claim perfection. We do not claim to make final judgments. We do not claim that we are above those whom we judge. We do, however, affirm that we are commanded to study the Scriptures to find the truth about two simple questions: What does God want us to believe and how does He want us to live? We affirm that we have the responsibility to live by these truths and encourage others to do the same.

Discernment, as we shall see, determines our destiny.

NOTES

1. George Barna, "Practical Outcomes Replace Biblical Principles As the Moral Standard," Barna Research Online, 10 September 2001. Accessed at www.barna.org.
2. D. Martyn Lloyd-Jones, *Studies in the Sermon on the Mount* (Grand Rapids: Eerdmans, 1960), 2:178–79.
3. Ibid., 177.
4. Ibid., 177–78.

3

WHEN YOU JUDGE DOCTRINE

*Does What
We Believe
Really Matter?*

"I don't care what you believe; I care about the way you live!"

That's what a churchgoer said when I asked him about his understanding of the gospel. He was impatient, he said, with those who quibbled about minor points of doctrine when there were such great needs in the world. "Doctrine" he said, "just gets in the way of the more important issues like integrity and compassion."

No doubt too much time has often been spent on doctrinal quibbles. But there can be no topic on planet Earth as important as the question of how one gets to heaven. The answer we give to that question determines our eternal destiny. Yes, of course, one can be a moral person without understanding the gospel; indeed, loosely defined, there are good people in all religions. But what one cannot do is go to heaven without a basic understanding of the gospel—at least that is what the Bible teaches.

Some churches have attracted large memberships by stressing "felt needs." Their leaders are committed to showing the relevance of Christianity to raising a good family, getting along with coworkers, and being successful in business. And since people have no felt need to listen to the gospel, its message often takes second place and is carefully slipped into discussions on relevant topics. What these well-intentioned ministers forget is that when we stand as sinners in the presence of God, our greatest felt need of the moment will be for the righteousness of Christ to shield us from God's holiness. Yes, of course, we should cater to felt needs, but we have to help people grasp what their felt needs *should* be.

> WHAT APPEARS GOOD ON THE SURFACE MAY NOT IN FACT BE ROOTED IN TRUTH.

Truth be told, we cannot get to heaven without the right beliefs; nor can we properly order our lives without right beliefs. What we believe about God will determine what we believe about ourselves; it will determine what we believe about others and what we believe about the purpose of our existence. Success today does not guarantee success in the hereafter. It is because of wrong doctrine that people will be lost forever. Sound doctrine determines a sound faith; a sound faith will guide us in this life and qualify us for the life to come. There is a connection between belief and behavior, between doctrine and destiny.

Of course doctrine divides; that is its purpose! But it also has another purpose: to unite the people of God around a common faith. We are to stand together in fellowship and be united against the heresies that ever try to subvert the faith. Danger comes when doctrine divides people who ought to be together.[1] But when it comes to the doctrine of salvation, *it is much better to be divided by truth than to be united by error.*

This brings us to the topic of doctrinal *discernment.* We've already used the word, but what does it mean? John MacArthur defines discernment as "the ability to distinguish truth from error" or, more accurately, "to distinguish truth from half-truths."[2] Error is usually easy to detect; but an encounter with a mixture of truth and error is more difficult to sort out.

A man walked into a meeting to observe a so-called laughing revival, with people on the floor, giggling and roaring like lions. He asked, half out loud, "I wonder whether this is really of God?" A woman standing beside him responded, "Well, it is happening in *church,* isn't it?" But it is precisely what is happening in church that should be tested and evaluated. It is in church where we can expect counterfeit miracles, odd beliefs, and heresy.

A sober evaluation of church history reveals that what appears good on the surface may not in fact be rooted in truth. There have been counterfeit healings, counterfeit revivals, and counterfeit gospel preaching. No wonder Paul told us, "Test everything. Hold on to the good. Avoid every kind of evil" (1 Thessalonians 5:21–22). We are commanded to do our best to distinguish the true from the false, and the true from the half-true.

The proliferation of talk shows, with their banality and trash, has helped our culture normalize the bizarre. Fringe behavior is extolled as if it is on the same continuum as that which is moral, acceptable, and decent. Homosexuals, transvestites, and prostitutes are paraded in front of national television audiences without objective moral judgments, except, of course, from the "radical religious right." Everyone is OK; no behavior is better than any other. It is difficult to overexaggerate the harm that such thinking has done in blurring important distinctions.

> THE WORDS OF THE FALSE PROPHET AND THE ITCHING EARS OF THE PEOPLE ARE IN SYNC.

Just as talk shows normalize fringe behavior, so many prophets and so-called faith healers have normalized bizarre experiences and doctrines. All kinds of ideas are expressed without rebuke or the slightest hint that they might be false. If God wants to heal a woman by having her head shaken for twenty minutes, who are we to judge? Any spoken revelation is believed to be from God, no matter whether it is contrary to Scripture or just plain silly.

Scriptures warn against false teachers and their doctrines. "For the time will come when men will not put up with sound doctrine. Instead, to suit their own desires, they will gather around them a great number of teachers to say what their itching ears want to hear" (2 Timothy 4:3). False teachers are driven by their desires and by their greed. People want to hear what pleases them; they will not want to have their sin exposed but will listen only to those with whom their desires agree. They will set themselves up as their own standard and then find someone to validate them.

Without rigorous submission to God's Word, people will develop a theology that will (1) allow them to justify their accumulation of wealth; (2) cater to their pride as God's special spokesmen; and (3) provide a context where immorality is condoned. Even if a false prophet should be exposed as a fraud, he will be able to continue because "God has forgiven him; why can't we?" In short, nothing will be allowed to stand against false teaching, a dubious lifestyle, and a hunger for power.

No wonder discernment is in such short supply! Weary of some of the excesses of past doctrinal conflicts and absorbed by the present passion for unity, we have succumbed to the spirit of the age. In our fear of being called unloving, we have allowed a climate to develop where every opinion is as valid as another. We are so afraid of being accused of discrimination that we have forgotten that we are to be *discriminating*. Love, it is said, forbids us to stand up and say, "This is false." So we must politely accept anyone who says, "The Lord told me that . . ."

Remember the story of the Trojan horse that was left outside the city of Troy? The would-be conquerors left it as a "gift" for the city, then disappeared in apparent retreat. A priest warned the citizens to not trust the enemy "even if he comes bearing gifts."

You know the rest of the story. After the wooden horse was brought into the city, soldiers jumped out and threw open the gates and the invaders swarmed in. Today the enemy is within our gates.

HOW HERESY FLOURISHES

The false teachers among us do not outrightly deny the teachings of the Bible, for to do so would greatly diminish their audience. Rather, they simply ignore the passages that

do not fit their agenda of unity, prosperity, and special revelation. By proclaiming disunity to be the greatest of sins, every doctrinal aberration imaginable is allowed to flourish.
Anyone who raises concerns about sound doctrine is quickly
silenced as a "heresy hunter" who should be shunned.
Much-needed voices are reduced to silence.

How are the false teachers able to dupe so many evan-
gelicals into their cause? They have adopted principles of
interpretation that allow them to take the Bible in hand and
twist it like putty into any shape they desire. Rather than
follow sound principles of interpretation, they "twist" the
Scriptures, as Peter warns in 2 Peter 3:16 (NKJV).

What are those wrong principles?

Old Testament Prosperity for New Testament Believers

Many take the Old Testament promises of blessing given
to Israel and apply them directly to the church without further ado. In the Old Testament, there was indeed a tight connection between the obedience of the people and the promise
that the land would produce good crops and wealth. Today,
however, this connection no longer exists for the simple reason that in this era God is not working with His people as belonging to a geographical nation. He has chosen to take out a
people for His name from within all the nations of the world,
forming a new body called the church. Thus, in the New
Testament, promises of spiritual blessing are given to those
who are faithful to the Lord, but there is no promise of
wealth or health. Indeed, we are promised poverty, persecution, and trials, just as Christ Himself experienced.

Disregarding these important distinctions, health and

wealth preachers have told their followers that they have a right to expect material blessings—especially if they are willing to send a large gift to the evangelist as "seed faith." Indeed, one evangelist claimed that if the people sent their credit card statements to him, he would burn them and God would miraculously deliver them from debt! This astounding claim was followed by testimonies of people who unexpectedly received huge checks in the mail to pay off their mortgages and the like. No need to make hard budget decisions; no need to trade in a new car for a used one: God will bail you out of debt—if you are willing to send the evangelist your "pledge of faith." Indeed, "if you plant the seed, the harvest is already there."

Anyone who questions this foolishness is told, "Who are you to say what God can or can't do?" The question, of course, is not what God can or cannot do; the question is whether this is what He promised and whether we have the right to insist that He fulfill that supposed promise.

Thus, under the guise of selected Scripture, without sound principles of interpretation, all of the desires of wealth and health are cloaked with verses of Scripture. The balanced teachings of the New Testament are ignored in favor of the Jesus-wants-you-rich syndrome. This teaching, of course, fits in perfectly with the materialistic aspirations of a large slice of the American pie. The words of the false prophet and the itching ears of the people are in sync.

In the early centuries, Christians held discussions on whether or not a rich person could even be saved. Contemporary prophets not only answer yes to the question but go on to say that it is God's will for everyone to be rich. Good-bye to the poverty of Jesus; good-bye to generations of the faithful who "went about in sheepskins and goatskins, destitute, persecuted and mistreated" (Hebrews 11:37). Goodbye to the faith of millions of Christians today who languish in prisons, unable to find food for their starving children.

Welcome to the world of contemporary prophets! Someone has said, "We have cows for milk; sheep for wool; and now we have God to satisfy our every craving!"

All Sickness and Poverty Is from the Devil

A second principle of interpretation that opened the floodgates to heresy was this reasoning: All sickness and poverty is from the devil. And, the argument went, since we have absolute power over the devil, it follows that we can "rebuke" all sickness and poverty and so be healthy and prosperous. All of this without repentance, without suffering for the sake of righteousness, and without the pursuit of the disciplines that lead to a holy life! Yes, all this and heaven too!

The fact is that the New Testament does not allow us to assume that all sickness and poverty is of the devil; and even when it is from the devil, we are given no assurance that we can overcome such ailments. Paul had a thorn in the flesh, a messenger of Satan to "buffet" him (2 Corinthians 12:7 KJV). Yet when he besought the Lord three times, God declined to deliver him but rather compensated by giving him grace to bear the trial (v. 9). Study the lives of the apostles, and you will not find one who was given wealth and health; most were given persecution, jail terms, and death.

Of course our authority over the devil is not absolute. We do not have authority to forbid him to work in Washington, D.C., as some people have thought. Nor do we have the authority to forbid him to run errands for God, as he did when Job was given a trial by the Lord (Job 1:12; 2:6). Yes, if we put on the armor of God we do have the power to overcome him in our individual lives and experience. But even then, God uses the Evil One to test us, tempt us, and otherwise teach us our need to stay close to the Lord, who redeemed us from the kingdom of darkness. Elsewhere I have written extensively on this topic.[3]

The Continuation of Revelation

Then came the final blow to any controls regarding doctrine. With the flowering of what is called the Faith Movement and thanks to some (but not all) in the charismatic movement, we have millions of people who believe that God speaks directly to the "prophets" of today; thus, serious Bible study is unnecessary. Prophets with fresh revelations from God have come to our churches with new messages filled with great promises and brimming with relevance.

Several years ago, there was what was called the Toronto Blessing, with people from all over Canada, the United States, and Britain flocking to a church near the Toronto airport, where people were known to bark like dogs, be "slain in the spirit," and be overcome by uncontrollable laughter. Since several books have been written about this movement, it is not my intention to evaluate it in depth, but I must quote the words of those who know the movement "from the inside out."

Three charismatic authors, who are generally sympathetic to manifestations of the Spirit, have written of their grave misgivings about what was happening in Toronto.

One of them, Peter Fenwick, wrote, "My greatest fear springs from the fact that the Bible no longer occupies the place which it once did in the evangelical community. Indeed, the whole controversy surrounding the Toronto Blessing is in fact a major battle for the Bible."[4] He goes on to say that the Toronto Blessing could not have started were it not for the acceptance of unbiblical practices.

When serious Bible students pointed out that the "word of knowledge" in the New Testament (1 Corinthians 12:8 KJV) does not refer to clairvoyance, that is, the ability of an evangelist to divine the various diseases of people in his audience, such instruction fell on deaf ears. For the most part, it did not matter what the leaders did or said; it did not matter whether their practices were bizarre or their doctrine new and inconsistent. The leaders responded to criticism by saying, "Who are you to question what God is doing?"

When people questioned why some things that were happening were not found in the Bible, the leaders responded with the verse "See, I am doing a new thing!" (Isaiah 43:19). Never mind that in the biblical context this "new thing" is God bringing the Jews back from exile, resettling them in the land, and establishing the coming kingdom. But this verse, wrested from its context, was now used to justify virtually anything and everything. Since now any manifestation of the Spirit could be described as a "new thing," Christians found themselves defenseless against error.

Today "new revelations" are received, the "prophet" saying, "The Spirit of God spoke to me and said . . . ," the sentence often being completed with all manner of foolishness and heresy. The notion that Jesus took upon Himself the nature of Satan, or the idea that Jesus was reborn in hell, or the heresy that we are all as divine as Jesus—such absurdities and a hundred like them have all been revealed to one or more of the self-styled prophets.[5] Millions believe.

Some time ago I received a letter from a friend who said that I made a remark on the radio that disturbed him deeply. When I read his letter, I knew I had not made the statement, because it was one with which I disagreed. Yet, because he insisted, I actually found a tape of the message to hear it for myself. I was relieved to discover that I was right; I had not made the comment attributed to me. He had made an inference based on a part of my message—an inference that misstated my position on the subject. My point is this: if I do not like it when people put words in my mouth, *how much more serious it must be to put words in the mouth of God!*

> TRUTH MIXED WITH ERROR IS SOMETIMES MORE DEADLY THAN ERROR ALL BY ITSELF.

Of course God still speaks to us today, if by that we mean that He reveals the sin in our hearts and illuminates our minds regarding the work of Christ on our behalf. Indeed, God may even grant special "acts of providence" to prepare people for the gospel. Some Muslims who have converted to Christianity tell us that they had dreams or visions of Jesus before they heard the gospel. There are times when God directs our throughts through prayer and meditation; or we may have impressions that give us guidance. But because we find it difficult to distinguish our thoughts from God's, it is much better to say, "I think the Lord is showing me . . . ," or, "It occurred to me . . ." This is quite different from saying that God gives prophecies, clairvoyance, and new doctrines. We dare not put our subjective thoughts on a par with canonical Scripture.

Since no movement in the history of the church is either entirely bad or entirely good, it goes without saying that some people have benefited from the Toronto Blessing and the teachings of the Faith Movement. Some have a new love for Christ, and others are encouraged in their walk with God. But cut off from serious biblical controls, such movements are allowed to go their own way, using the Scripture willy-nilly to justify their absurdities.

Flip through the channels of your television set and you will find many evangelists who, in effect, teach that the more bizarre something is, the more likely it is believed to be of God.

You will find extravagant promises of healing; there are signs, wonders, laughter, and reports of teeth filled with gold fillings; you will hear stories of money coming quite literally out of nowhere to "bless" those who have sent in a gift. And, to make matters more confusing, in the midst of all of this, helpful scriptural truth is sometimes proclaimed.

Let it be clearly said that if we want to find the devil in America we must begin by looking behind the pulpits of America; it is in the church and not in the world that the devil does his most deceptive work. Truth mixed with error is sometimes more deadly than error all by itself.

RECYCLED HERESIES

Heresies of various kinds are not new. During the Reformation there was a prophet named Thomas Munster, who believed that the Bible was too difficult to interpret. It needed a divine interpreter—and that was not the church but the inward witness of the Spirit. The Bible, he declared, was but paper and ink. "Bible, Babel, bubble!" he cried.[6] Using the same Scripture as modern self-styled prophets, he justified his doctrinal position with the statement "For the letter kills, but the Spirit gives life" (2 Corinthians 3:6). Luther replied, that yes, of course, the letter without the spirit was dead, but the two are to be no more divorced than the soul is to be separated from the body. Luther said he needed a sure word from God, not the fantastic experiences of a modern-day prophet.

As for Munster's dreams, visions, and revelations, Luther, remembering that the Holy Spirit is represented in the Bible as a dove, said he would not listen to Munster even if "he had swallowed the Holy Ghost, feathers and all."[7] Munster became the father of all those who believed in the infusion of the Spirit that bypasses the Scriptures.

The Bible properly interpreted does not allow us to twist its teachings to suit our desires. If we interpret it fairly, it will not allow us to believe anything and everything. As Jay Adams says, the Bible engages in what could be called antithetical teaching:

> In the Bible, where antithesis is so important, discern-
> ment—the ability to distinguish God's thoughts and
> God's ways from all others—is essential. Indeed, God
> says that "the wise in heart will be called discerning"
> (Proverbs 16:21).
>
>   From the Garden of Eden with its two trees (one al-
> lowed, one forbidden) to the eternal destiny of the hu-

man being in heaven or in hell, the Bible sets forth two, and only two, ways: God's way, and all others. Accordingly, people are said to be saved or lost. They belong to God's people or the world. There was Gerizim, the mount of blessing, and Ebal, the mount of cursing. There is the narrow way and the wide way, leading either to eternal life or to destruction. There are those who are against and those who are with us, those within and those without. There is life and death, truth and falsehood, good and bad, light and darkness, the kingdom of God and the kingdom of Satan, love and hatred, spiritual wisdom and the wisdom of the world. Christ is said to be the way, the truth, and the life, and no one may come to the Father but by Him. His is the only name under the sky by which we may be saved.[8]

UNITY/DISUNITY

So where do we draw the line? When do we know whether a doctrine is worth fighting for? Surely we would agree that differences in our understanding prophecy is no reason to cry "heresy." I was brought up with the teaching that the church will be raptured before the Tribulation period. But many of my friends who believe God's Word as deeply as I do are convinced that the church will go through the Tribulation (although, I'm sure they secretly hope they are wrong!).

Our problem is one of balance. On the one hand, some among us draw the doctrinal circle too narrowly. They break fellowship with anyone who does not hold to their views *exactly*. Some insist that we all use the King James Version of the Bible; others believe that only those who hold to some form of "second blessing" theology are truly filled with the Spirit. It is fine to have such convictions, as long as it is understood that these are not the fundamentals; these are not the issues over which we must break fellowship with one another. I hold to many of the convictions of what is popularly called Calvinism, with its emphasis on God's sovereignty and predestination; others are more akin to Arminianism, with its emphasis on free will. But these should not be the matters over which we divide, nor should they define heresy.

What about an issue such as baptism? I'm convinced that the Bible teaches believer's baptism, that is, the baptism of those who can consciously bear witness to their faith in Christ. I also believe that the proper form of baptism is immersion in water. But if someone believes in sprinkling or pouring water on the head, such differences, though important, are not matters to cause division.

What should be said about infant baptism? Some interpret it as a sign of the covenant, that is, a sign that the infant is included within the sphere of God's blessing of salvation. I'm not sure I understand exactly what this means (is it a sign that the child will some day be saved? or is it a sign that the parents promise to raise the child for Christ?), but I can respect their viewpoint.

However, there are many who teach that baptism actually is the means of salvation. The liturgies of the Catholic and Lutheran churches teach that baptism effects regeneration; indeed, if an infant is born sickly, a priest or minister will rush to the hospital so that there can be a baptism before death. In extreme cases, the mother herself might perform the baptism; or a member of the hospital staff might do so.

Though both Catholics and Lutherans believe that baptism must be updated through confirmation, they hold that a child is initially saved through this ritual. For some of us, this is a serious deviation from biblical teaching.

Others hold to a variation of these views. Some believe that faith in Christ is necessary for salvation, but that such faith is of no value apart from baptism. In fact, the Boston Church of Christ teaches not only that one must be baptized to be saved but that only their church's baptism counts for salvation.[9] One of their number told me that although I had been baptized, I was going to hell because I was not baptized by them. Given these interpretations of baptism, a proper understanding of the doctrine of baptism is worth fighting for.

What is heresy?

The Bible uses the word *heresy* and *heretic* in two senses. Paul referred to various factions as "heresies," that is, "divisions" (see 1 Corinthians 11:19 in the KJV and NIV). Some of these divisions are between believers; defined in this way, a carnal believer who refuses to accept revealed truth can be called a heretic. This, I believe, is how Paul used the word in Galatians 5:19–20, when he said that heresies (KJV), or factions (NIV), are the work of the flesh. Elsewhere he said that a heretic (KJV), or divisive person (NIV), is perverted and self-condemned (Titus 3:10–11).

The second use of the word refers to those who hold to serious doctrinal deviations. Peter speaks of "destructive heresies" that deny that Jesus is Lord (2 Peter 2:1). These are teachers who deny the basic doctrines of the faith, and this is how we use the word most often today. Robert Bowman, in *Orthodoxy and Heresy,* defines heresy as "a teaching which directly opposes the essentials of the Christian faith, so that true Christians must divide themselves from those who hold it."[10]

Can Christians become heretics? Certainly they can be called heretics according to the first definition given above. And often Christians have held to heretical ideas, either due to ignorance or personal rebellion. In a few instances, some who actually professed the evangelical faith have

> WE ARE NOT LEFT TO DECIDE ON OUR OWN WHERE THE LINE BETWEEN TRUTH AND ERROR SHOULD BE DRAWN.

turned aside to destroy the faith they once held, either by their lifestyle or by advocating myths and traditions that undermine the faith they once affirmed. Yes, they too are heretics.

RETURNING TO THE BASICS

To "do theology," as the saying goes, we must engage in antithetical thinking. That means that if we *affirm* a doctrine, we must also *deny* its opposite. Such reasoning is the basis for all rationality; it is a necessary function of the human mind. Not only that, such reasoning is consistent with the teachings of the Bible.

For example, let's take the statement "The Bible alone is God's Word to us." If that statement is true, it excludes other sources of revelation and authorities. It excludes the traditions of Roman Catholicism as a means of revelation; it excludes the Book of Mormon, the Koran, and the Vedas. It also excludes the writings of Mary Ellen White and those of Mary Baker Eddy.

Those of us who believe that the Bible is God's only source of revelation expect no more revelation to come through the lips of gurus, prophets, evangelists, and revivalists. No one will ever be able to claim that God has revealed something new about the Holy Spirit; or something new about Christ; or something new about prophecy. Of course, we believe that there might be a better way to explain what God has revealed; there might be deeper understanding, but we are limited to the words of God on the pages of Scripture. If someone says, "The Lord told me," we might find his claim interesting; at times a person might be right about the impression he has received, but we do not take this "revelation" as the inerrant Word of God.

Once we accept the Bible as the only basis for all doctrine, we find that the Bible itself helps us define what doctrines are nonnegotiable. We are not left to decide on our own where the line between truth and error should be drawn. Throughout the New Testament we are constantly confronted with the doctrine of salvation, and the cluster of doctrines that support it, to be of utmost importance. This makes sense when you realize that the most important question we could ever have answered is how we can be sure that we will spend eternity with God.

Paul warned the believers in Galatia that some among them were trying to pervert the gospel of Christ. Then he added, "But even if we or an angel from heaven should preach a gospel other than the one we preached to you, let him be eternally condemned! As we have already said, so now I say again: If anybody is preaching to you a gospel other than what you accepted, let him be eternally condemned!" (Galatians 1:8–9).

Imagine! An angel comes and tells us that the way to heaven is to be a loving, decent person. You'd be surprised at how many would believe such a revelation. Proof of this is that the Book of Mormon was revealed by an "angel" who gave a revelation of an entirely different gospel to Joseph Smith, and millions have believed the message. There have been apparitions of Mary with a different gospel, and shrines have been built in honor of her appearance. Or, for that matter, there have been revelations of Jesus with a different gospel. Paul would say, "Let such revelations be accursed!"

Paul "got into Peter's face" about just giving a wrong *impression* about the gospel. What happened was this: Peter backed off from eating with the Gentiles when the Judaizers appeared on the scene, giving the impression that he sided with these teachers, who held that we are saved through Christ plus the Law. To our knowledge, Peter never said a word about the content of the gospel; he just refused to eat with those who believed that the gospel was a free gift of God by faith.

Paul was livid! Peter's simply giving the impression that the Judaizers might be right was enough for Paul to confront him publicly.

> *When Peter came to Antioch, I opposed him to his face, because he was clearly in the wrong. . . .*
>
> *When I saw that they were not acting in line with the truth of the gospel, I said to Peter in front of them all, "You are a Jew, yet you live like a Gentile and not like a Jew. How is it, then, that you force Gentiles to follow Jewish customs?" (Galatians 2:11, 14)*

Paul then went on to affirm that we are justified through faith in Christ and not the works of the Law (v. 16). Make no mistake: The clarity of the gospel is the one doctrine for which we should be willing to give our lives.

What is this gospel? Is it simply "believe on Jesus"? No, for as we shall see in the next chapter, there are many false cults who also "believe on Jesus." The whole cluster of doctrines that form a part of the doctrine of salvation must all be held together as a part of the divine scheme.

To illustrate how to "do theology," I shall outline the basic doctrines of the gospel but also show what is denied by what is affirmed. In the process, we undercut almost all heresies, ancient and modern. Older theologians wisely used affirmations and denials as a means to clarify what the truth was believed to be. Let us see how this method might be applied.

PROPOSITIONS OF THE GOSPEL

Here I delineate the basic propositions of the evangelical faith, showing what it includes and excludes.

1. *We affirm that God is holy.* This means that God is separate, distinct, pure, and "wholly other," that is, wholly apart from His creatures.

Why is this an important part of the gospel? Because if God were unholy, He could receive sinners without a sacrifice. Many popular books on the topic of spirituality speak as if God can be approached directly by anyone at any time in any way. The God presented is really no different from us; perhaps a bit more powerful, but not holy. Thus, there is no need for fear in his or her presence. No need for an atonement. Such a god is not the God of the Bible.

Nor is the god of civil religion the God of the Bible. After the terrorist attack on September 11, "God Bless America" signs went up all over America. Many Christians were glad that "God was back" in American life. I was not convinced. Indeed, I was told that two adult book and video stores (porn shops) in Nashville had on their marquee, "God bless America." But this was a reference to a different god, the god of modern hedonism, not the God who said, "Be holy, because I am holy" (Leviticus 11:44–45).

> OUR SINFULNESS PRECLUDES ANY CONTACT WITH GOD ON OUR OWN INITIATIVE.

We also deny that the God of the Bible is the same as Allah, or the gods of Buddhism, Hinduism, and other religions. We deny that it is possible to reach God without accepting His own righteousness as our own as found in Christ (see below).

2. *We affirm that Jesus is God in the flesh.* Listen to the warning of John, the apostle of love.

> *Dear friends, do not believe every spirit, but test the spirits to see whether they are from God, because many false prophets have gone out into the world. This is how you can recognize the Spirit of God: Every spirit that acknowledges that Jesus Christ has come in the flesh is from God, but every spirit that does not acknowledge Jesus is not from God. This is the spirit of the antichrist, which you have heard is coming and even now is already in the world.* (1 John 4:1–3)

Other passages affirming the deity of Christ are found in many places (see, for example, John 1:1; Hebrews 1:8).

To deny the deity and incarnation of Christ is clear proof of a heretic; however, affirming these doctrines is not

necessarily proof of orthodoxy. Some who believe these doctrines nevertheless teach salvation by works, or they add
their righteousness to what Jesus accomplished. But to affirm the deity of Christ and His incarnation, we therefore
exclude other popular doctrines.

We deny that Jesus of Nazareth can be separated from
Christ; we deny that there is a Gnostic or Universal Christ
who is found within all religions. We also deny the doctrine
of the Jehovah's Witnesses, who teach that Christ is a created
being. We must reject the teachings of the Jesus Seminar,
which asserts that Christ is a mere man.

As you might know, these scriptural doctrines put us in
direct conflict with Islam, which teaches that the Incarnation
is blasphemy. In dialogue with Muslims, we must remember, however, that their aversion to the Incarnation is based
on the mistaken notion that Christianity holds to a physical
trinity. Thus, to a Muslim, to claim that Jesus is the Son of
God means that the Father had sex with Mary and the result
was "the Son of God." We must point out that we believe in
a spiritual trinity, not a physical one.

3. *We affirm the substitutionary atonement.* Peter wrote,
"Christ died for sins once for all, the righteous for the un-
righteous, to bring you to God" (1 Peter 3:18). This means
that Christ suffered for us on the cross to become our sin
bearer. He took the penalty that we deserved and paid the
debt of those who would take advantage of His sacrifice.

We deny that God can save us because of His love, quite
apart from the sacrifice of Christ. We also deny that there
are other mediators between us and God, whether dead
saints or angels. We also deny that Mohammed, Krishna, or

any other guru, teacher, or prophet is qualified to die in our stead and thus bring us to God.

4. *We affirm that we are sinners by nature and by choice.* Paul wrote, "As for you, you were dead in your transgressions and sins" (Ephesians 2:1). Our sinfulness precludes any contact with God on our own initiative. All of our good deeds, though good in themselves, are nevertheless tainted with sin. We are incapable of making any contribution to our salvation.

We deny all forms of works-salvation, whether found in Catholicism or non-Christian religions. We deny the perfectibility of human nature and the belief that God is obligated to save us because of our inherent goodness.

5. *We affirm that the means of receiving salvation is faith alone.* "We maintain that a man is justified by faith apart from observing the law" (Romans 3:28). It follows that salvation has to be a free gift because the righteousness we need is that of which we have none. Thus we are saved by accepting Christ as the One who paid the penalty for our sin.

We deny that salvation is mediated through the sacraments, whether baptism, Communion, and the like. We deny that the gift of salvation becomes ours through a process of cooperation between us and God.

6. *We affirm that assurance of salvation comes through resting in the sufficiency of Christ's work in our behalf.*

And this is the testimony: God has given us eternal life, and this life is in his Son. He who has the Son has life; he who does not have the Son of God does not have life. I write these things to you who believe in the name of the Son of God so that you may know that you have eternal life. (1 John 5:11–13)

We deny that assurance is based upon our works, except insofar as our works give evidence of saving faith. We deny that we can have assurance through any rituals of the church or our own sincerity and good works. If we believe that when Jesus died and rose again He did everything that will be necessary to be received into the presence of a holy God; if we embrace what He did for us, we will be saved and know it.

POSTSCRIPT

How do you know when a postmodern man is actually converted to Christ? Not when he says he believes in Jesus, for even the demons believe and tremble. Not when he says that he has accepted Christ as his Savior, since many believe that they have done so through the sacraments or through their own efforts.

We know that a man understands the gospel when he (1) admits that he is a sinner and cannot make any contribution to his salvation; (2) affirms that he has accepted Christ because He alone has the only righteousness God accepts; and (3) says that he knows that Christ is, therefore, the only way to the Father.

There is a story about a young child who was lost in a big city. When the policeman asked him his address, he could not answer. The lad knew only his name. He did say, however, that if they could take him to his church he could find his way home from there. "But which church?" they asked. He replied, "The one with the big cross on the front!" Then he added, "Just take me to the cross, and I will find my way home!"

Discerning Christians will test teachers, prophets, and evangelists by the clarity with which they preach the gospel of the Cross. And if the gospel is distorted or ignored, we can be quite sure that we have encountered a teacher who is not to be followed. For only the Cross, properly understood, can take us home to the Father.

In an age of confusion, we must contend for the basics.

NOTES

1. Robert Bowman Jr., *Orthodoxy and Heresy: A Biblical Guide to Doctrinal Discernment* (Grand Rapids: Baker, 1992), 17.
2. John F. MacArthur Jr., "Discernment—Spiritual Survival for a Church in Crisis," tape series (n.d.).
3. Erwin W. Lutzer, *The Serpent of Paradise: The Incredible Story of How Satan's Rebellion Serves God's Purposes* (Chicago: Moody, 1996).
4. Clifford Hill, Peter Fenwick, David Forbes, and David Noakes, *Blessing the Church?* (Guildford, Surrey [U.K.]: Eagle, 1995), 40–41.
5. Hank Hanegraaff, *Christianity in Crisis* (Eugene, Oreg.: Harvest, 1993). This is an excellent exposition of the teachings and heresies of what is called the Faith Movement. Must reading for those who are serious about discernment in this age of revelations, prophecies, miracles, and foolishness.
6. Rolland Bainton, *Here I Stand: A Life of Martin Luther* (New York & Toronto: Mentor, 1950), 203.
7. Ibid.
8. Jay Adams, *A Call to Discernment* (Eugene, Oreg.: Harves, 1987), 31; quoted by John F. MacArthur in *Reckless Faith: When the Church Loses Its Will to Discern* (Wheaton, Ill.: Crossway, 1994), 49–50.
9. Russ Wise, "The Boston Church," www.probe.org/docs/boston.html; see also www.reveal.org/abouticc/crossroadsera.html.
10. Bowman, *Orthodoxy and Heresy*, 50.

4

WHEN YOU JUDGE FALSE PROPHETS

How Can We Recognize Them?

B eware of false prophets."
With that statement, Jesus affirms two truths: first that there are false prophets, and second, that they are dangerous. As people become more accustomed to gravitating to preachers who tell them what they want to hear, we should not be surprised that false prophets are everywhere. Many of them have wide followings, and their lifestyles are supported by earnest Christians.

We've been told that we should not investigate miracles, prophecies, or teachings because this divides the body of Christ. Some warn that we should not touch "the Lord's anointed" lest we fall under the judgment of God. But we must keep in mind that this warning refers to protecting the Lord's servants from physical harm and has nothing to do with identifying false teachers and their doctrines (see

1 Chronicles 16:22; Psalm 105:15). Our intention in this chapter is not to do harm to the Lord's servants but rather to expose those who would lead the people of God astray. We are not intimidated by television evangelists who pronounce a curse on all those who would expose their teachings and unbiblical practices. Wolves are preying on the sheep, and we have to sound an alarm.

We have underestimated the ability of Satan's messengers to position themselves as the Lord's ministers. We must reread what the Scripture has to say about prophets who speak their own delusions rather than the words of God.

Two Kinds of False Prophets

The first class of false prophets is those whose predictions fail; that is, they claim special knowledge and announce things that do not come to pass. These are described by Moses.

> You may say to yourselves, "How can we know when a message has not been spoken by the LORD?" If what a prophet proclaims in the name of the LORD does not take place or come true, that is a message the LORD has not spoken. That prophet has spoken presumptuously. Do not be afraid of him. (Deuteronomy 18:21–22)

Because God knows the future infallibly, we can be sure that those who receive their messages from Him will always be correct in their predictions. A false prediction is a sure mark of a false prophet.

This principle, which is clearly taught in the Old Testament, also applies to New Testament prophets, including men such as the prophet Agabus (Acts 21:10–11). The bottom line is that any prophet in any era who speaks by the inspiration of God will be right in his predictions 100 percent of the time.

Incredibly, some people are so gullible that they will follow a prophet even if his predictions do not come to pass! Some Word of Faith preachers have claimed revelations about impending miracles and coming revivals that have failed to come to pass and have shared heretical visions. Yet, their followers are undeterred; they just keep attending the meetings and sending their money. Clearly, if a prophet predicts the future inaccurately, he has not heard from God.

The second kind of prophet is one who predicts the future accurately and does miracles but is still a heretic because of his false doctrines.

> If a prophet, or one who foretells by dreams, appears among you and announces to you a miraculous sign or wonder, and if the sign or wonder of which he has spoken takes place, and he says, "Let us follow other gods" (gods you have not known) "and let us worship them," you must not listen to the words of that prophet or dreamer. The LORD your God is testing you to find out whether you love him with all your heart and with all your soul. (Deuteronomy 13:1–3)

In other words, *even if the prophecy comes to pass, this in itself does not prove that the prophet has been sent by God.* We have to know more about his theology before we can approve of his revelations.

Do we have a scriptural example of this second kind of false prophet? Balaam (Numbers 22–24) was an occultist who was asked by the king of Moab to curse the Israelites.

Such diviners of the day had great influence, and it was believed that those they cursed would be cursed and whomever they blessed would be blessed. So a pagan king asked a pagan prophet to curse Israel. The princes of the king went to Balaam with money in their hands, and he was glad to oblige.

But try as he might, Balaam could not curse Israel. He opened his mouth to curse, but blessings came out! The king was displeased and told Balaam he'd better change his message if he expected to receive his promised bribe. False prophets often have an eye for money, lots of it (22:17).

Balaam tried to curse Israel a second time, a third, and a fourth. Yet nothing but blessing was on his lips. He made this astounding prophecy: "I see him, but not now; I behold him, but not near. A star will come out of Jacob; a scepter will rise out of Israel. He will crush the foreheads of Moab, the skulls of all the sons of Sheth" (24:17). You can imagine how exasperated the king of Moab became!

> A CORRECT PREDICTION DOES NOT AUTOMATICALLY PROVE THAT THE MAN OR WOMAN IS TO BE FOLLOWED.

His favorite prophet blessed his enemy! And in his blessings, Balaam gave some of the most beautiful prophecies about Israel that one can imagine.

Was Balaam a false prophet? His predictions came to pass, so he appears to have been a man of God. But there is no evidence that he changed his ways and became a follower of the true God. This explains why he is strongly condemned in the New Testament as one who is a prototype of all false prophets. Just listen to this:

With eyes full of adultery, they never stop sinning; they seduce the un-
stable; they are experts in greed—an accursed brood! They have left
the straight way and wandered off to follow the way of Balaam son of
Beor, who loved the wages of wickedness. But he was rebuked for his
wrongdoing by a donkey—a beast without speech—who spoke with a
man's voice and restrained the prophet's madness. (2 Peter 2:14–16)

Balaam had two characteristics that often distinguish a
false prophet. First, he was greedy; he could be bought if
the price was right. Second, and more important, though he
apparently was receiving true revelations from God, he had
not renounced his sorcery. "Now when Balaam saw that it
pleased the LORD to bless Israel, he did not resort to sorcery
as at other times, but turned his face toward the desert"
(Numbers 24:1). Though he could not curse Israel, he hit
on a plan to please the king and get his money: he later per-
suaded Israel to engage in sexual immorality with the
Moabite women and worship the pagan god Baal (31:16;
see also 25:1–3). It is no coincidence that the king took Balaam to the mountain of Peor (23:27–28); and it was at the
same mountain that we read, "So Israel joined in worship-
ing the Baal of Peor" (25:3).

There is a lesson here: It is not enough to ask whether
the prophet's predictions come to pass; it is not even enough
to ask whether he has, at times, spoken the words of God.
We must also ask about his lifestyle and, above all, his doctrines. No wonder Jesus said that false Christs will do so
many miracles that if possible they would deceive the elect
(Mark 13:22)!

My wife and I met a young man named Phil who told us
about attending a meeting of two or three thousand people,

where a priest said, "A young man is here fighting leukemia." Phil was fighting leukemia but thought that in a crowd of a few thousand there probably were several young men fighting leukemia. But then the priest continued, "This man is also going through a divorce." Phil thought, *Well, that is "two for two."* Then the leader predicted that this young man would have chemo and radiation treatments and then return "next September to testify to answered prayer." And that is what happened: Phil had chemo, along with a bone marrow transplant, and returned the next September to testify to his perfect healing.

Was this priest a true prophet of God? I don't think so. Though an inaccurate prediction disqualifies a prophet, a correct prediction does not automatically prove that the man or woman is to be followed. I asked Phil a question that led me to believe that the priest was a false prophet, even though what he predicted came to pass. Later in this chapter I will share with you the question I asked.

There are two different kinds of false prophets and four different kinds of false prophecies. "The prophets are prophesying lies in my name. I have not sent them or appointed them or spoken to them. They are prophesying to you *false visions, divinations, idolatries* and the *delusions* of their own minds" (Jeremiah 14:14, emphasis added).

- *False visions* may come from the heart of a false prophet or from Satan himself. These visions are actually "seen" by the prophet but they are false and devilish. I think of a woman, a self-proclaimed prophetess, who had a vision of the man one of her children would marry. She believed that this was a revelation from God to her mind, but the vision was misleading and it did not come to pass.

- *Divinations* may refer to palm reading and the like.
- *Idolatries* refers to those prophets who lead people to worship other gods or ask them to bow before graven images. Or perhaps they encourage the worship of a god who is the figment of their imagination.
- *Delusions,* which also might not be from the devil but instead be fabricated from within the mind of the prophet who himself believes his silly revelations.

Despite the large following of the prophets who said they were prophesying in His name, God said that He "did not send them" (14:15).

What were these prophets prophesying? Exactly what the people wanted to hear! They were saying that there would be neither war nor famine in the land, but that there would be prosperity (14:13). They argued that since the Israelites were the people of God, they should claim their inheritance. We can almost hear them say, "Let's not let the devil rob us of what is rightfully ours. We belong to Jehovah, God of the Universe; let us live accordingly!"

Yet, God said that they themselves would be destroyed by famine or sword (14:15–16). Elsewhere in Jeremiah, God says, "I have heard what the prophets say who prophesy lies in my name. They say, 'I had a dream! I had a dream!' How long will this continue in the hearts of these lying prophets, who prophesy the delusions of their own minds?" (23:25–26). No wonder the Lord says, "Do not listen to what the prophets are prophesying to you; they fill you with false hopes" (v. 16).

Now listen to the bottom line: "'The house of Israel and the house of Judah have been utterly unfaithful to me,' declares the LORD. They have lied about the LORD; they said, 'He will do nothing! No harm will come to us; we will never see sword or famine. The prophets are but wind and the word is not in them; so let what they say be done to them'" (5:11–13).

The prophets are but wind! They speak delusions from their own minds! They are filling the people with false hopes! That is what God says *false* prophets do (see v. 14). They claim to have knowledge that is denied to the rest of us. They claim to receive messages from God directly, unfiltered. Today, in extreme cases, they will actually ignore the Bible in favor of fresh revelations. They claim to have power; to have the ability to perform "signs and wonders." And the people believe them.

RECOGNIZING FALSE PROPHETS

We are struck by the similarities between the false prophets in the Scriptures and the false prophets of today. The first-century church was infiltrated with false teachers of various kinds, men who claimed to have special revelations from God. Paul describes them as "super-apostles," who believed themselves to be superior to the apostle Paul (2 Corinthians 11:5). They were apostles who gained acceptance by using letters of recommendation and claiming to lead the Corinthians into a fuller relationship with God. They did not dispute the need for faith in Christ; rather, they said that if you become Jewish, you will get all that God has for you.

These apostles presented themselves as wiser than Paul because they appealed to the felt needs of the people in a way that Paul did not. They had the key to a deeper spirituality by presenting a more complete message. Paul, they believed, had only a part of the truth, whereas they had all of it. They were also orators who could present their ideas with conviction and style. They had hidden knowledge, special insights, and new revelations. Paul's gospel appeared weak in comparison; indeed, his presence was almost an embarrassment to them. They said of him, "His letters are weighty and forceful, but in person he is unimpressive and his speaking amounts to nothing" (2 Corinthians 10:10).

> MANY PROCLAIM A JESUS WHO WILL GIVE YOU GIFTS AND BLESSINGS.

Today there are many prophets and teachers on television, and it is our responsibility to distinguish the false from the true, or at least the false from the half-true. We are not infallible, and in some instances we might have to simply admit that we do not have enough information to make a judgment. Yet because Jesus warned us about the proliferation of false teachers and because some are so flagrantly out of line with biblical teaching, we must ask: By what criteria are they to be judged?

Suppose we are watching an evangelist or miracle worker on television. What criteria might we use to determine whether this man or woman is authentic, a spiritual leader to be followed and supported? Let me encourage you to open your Bible to 2 Corinthians 11 and follow along as we consider Paul's description of the false teachers of his day. This will serve as a guide to discern the true teacher from the false one;

or, we could say, to discern the truth from the half-truths all of us have heard. Here are some of their characteristics.

They Have Their Own Jesus

Paul writes, "For if someone comes to you and preaches a Jesus other than the Jesus we preached, or if you receive a different spirit from the one you received . . ." (v. 4). Who was this Jesus whom the super-apostles preached? They believed that Jesus died on the cross but that His work was not enough; one had to become Jewish and add the works of the Law to what Christ had done. And, if one became Jewish, Christianity would really work; only then could one enter into the deeper things of God.

They did not deny what Paul taught; they just want to add to his message. Scott Hafeman, who has studied 2 Corinthians in detail, says that the teachers taught that because Jesus suffered, we do not have to.[1] Rather than seeing Jesus as a model of how to suffer, they believed Jesus suffered in our stead and thus exempted us from all suffering. Redemption meant entering into the fullness of the earthly blessings Jesus purchased for us on the cross. The false teachers taught that the blessings of heaven could be ours today.

If we are to enjoy life and prosper, we need two things. First, we need our health, since it is impossible to live a full life with physical ailments. Second, we need wealth, so that our needs (and desires) are met without interruption. The Jesus of the false prophets suffered not so much to redeem us from our sins but to purchase for us the blessings of heaven *now*. If one would just take a further step and become Jewish, the full blessings of the Spirit would be experienced.

Paul says, to the contrary, that any such teaching that adds to the Cross is the preaching of "another Jesus."

At Chicago's O'Hare Airport, I met a woman reading *The Prayer of Jabez,* so I asked her about her religious convictions. She said that she was a Mormon and was reading the book because she was beginning a new business and wanted God to bless it. When I told her that she must trust Christ, she said, "Jesus . . . we all serve Jesus, and there is only one Jesus, isn't there?"

No, I explained, there are many Jesuses in the world. The New Age Movement believes in the Cosmic Jesus who indwells everyone. There is the "Santa Claus" Jesus of some preachers, who gives blessings to all without discrimination, regardless of a person's religion or lifestyle. The great humanitarian Albert Schweitzer wrote a book in which he said that he believed Jesus was delusional. That surely was "another Jesus."

The false Jesus of Paul's day was not off in a corner, the creation of some strange cult. This was a Jesus that was proclaimed, a Jesus that was evidently preached within the church. *This Jesus was enough like the true Jesus that Paul feared that the people could not tell the difference.*

Many proclaim a Jesus who will give you gifts and blessings; he is the Jesus of prosperity, the Jesus who heals, the Jesus who loves everyone in the same way and never would send anyone to hell. What they do not emphasize is the Jesus who died on the cross to reconcile us to God, the One who will return in judgment upon all who do not obey the gospel.

These false prophets talk endlessly about Jesus. They will pray in the name of Jesus; they do miracles in the name of Jesus. They preach a Jesus who will give you benefits without repentance; a Jesus who will bless everyone no matter what they believe. They preach a Jesus who does not call us to suffer, but rather a Jesus who is "there for us," ready to bestow the blessings that will negate any suffering that has come our way. This Jesus will give you money, remove your problems, and do practically any miracle you ask for. There is a sensual Jesus; an entertainment Jesus.

What makes these prophets so insidious, Paul says, is that they have "a different spirit"; that is, they actually are controlled by an alien spirit. In some instances, a demon lurks behind their teaching, for they use their charisma to appear to exalt Jesus, yet their teachings are misguided. We must keep in mind that the Jesus we *want* is not necessarily the Jesus we *need.*

K. Neil Foster tells the story of a woman seeking help because she was overcome by a spirit that identified itself as Jesus. This "Jesus" threw her on the floor and bragged that it had control over a certain congregation in a certain city. This spirit hated the Lord Jesus Christ but was driven out by that name—the Lord Jesus Christ. Obviously, there are spirits that will take the name *Jesus* to confuse and deceive.[2]

How do we detect this "other Jesus"? As you watch and listen to a pastor, evangelist, or prophet, ask: Is the preaching of the Cross central to his ministry? Does he emphasize the need for repentance, holiness, and submission to God? Does he preach a Jesus who calls us to suffer, with the promise that He will walk with us through the suffering? Or does he present a Jesus whose primary function is to give us the blessings of heaven right now?

Sometimes there might not be a simple answer to these questions. There are teachers who actually refer to the gospel from time to time; or in a few instances they might preach both the message of the Cross and the message of earthly prosperity as if the two can coexist. In some cases, we must simply distinguish the true from what is half-true and withhold personal judgment. At other times, the "other Jesus" evangelists are easy for all to see.

They Have Their Own Gospel

If you have your own Jesus, it follows that you have your own gospel. "If someone comes to you and preaches a Jesus other than the Jesus we preached . . . or a *different gospel* from the one you accepted . . ." (2 Corinthians 11:4). We have already learned that the gospel of these "super-apostles" was the gospel of prosperity. And, in order to show that they "put their money where their mouth is," they did not preach without charging a fee. In fact, they argued that if Paul were really a great man he would not preach without reimbursement. So Paul had to defend the fact that he came and preached the gospel freely.

In defense of his "no charge" policy, Paul wrote, "Was it a sin for me to lower myself in order to elevate you by preaching the gospel of God to you free of charge? I robbed other churches by receiving support from them so as to serve you" (vv. 7–8). Paul said that he did not want to be a burden to the congregation, so he used funds he received from other churches to support himself, and of course, he worked with his own hands. Perhaps this was appreciated by the people, but the false teachers used this against Paul, arguing that he didn't charge because he was not as great a preacher as they.

Today the super-apostles emphasize that you should send them money for your own personal benefit. The more generous you are, the more God will open the windows of heaven to give you benefits you "will not have room to receive." They hide their greed under the rubric of giving their adherents an opportunity to be blessed of God. In effect the message is, "Don't you see how fortunate you are to send me your money!"

Why has this gospel of prosperity found such a ready acceptance in the hearts of millions of Americans? First, because like the prophets of Israel, modern-day preachers have found a message people want to hear. No need to speak about the hard aspects of the Christian life; no need to carry one's cross or to bear up under suffering. No need for turning from sin or choosing to live without creature comforts.

Of course, these apostles will quote the Bible, claiming to believe it "from cover to cover." But they will omit the passages that do not fit with their mind-set. I heard one false prophet actually say, "This business of Jesus dying for us . . . I'm not interested in what Jesus did two thousand years ago; I'm interested in the blessings he gives me today." In the mind of this man, our problem is not sin but ignorance; we just don't know how to access God and get our inheritance.

A second reason for this wide acceptance of the prosperity gospel is its appeal to greed. Peter describes the preachers of his day: "In their greed these teachers will exploit you with *stories they have made up*. Their condemnation has long been hanging over them, and their destruction has not been sleeping" (2 Peter 2:3, emphasis added). One television preacher said that some who sent him money received letters from the mortgage company saying that their loan was fully paid! *Stories they have made up!*

The early church said that one of the ways they recognized a false prophet was if someone came to their church seeking money. As we have learned, Paul said he had the right to ask for money (2 Corinthians 9) but refused, so as not to be a stumbling block for them. He used a bit of irony; yes, he said, he was a robber; he robbed other churches so that he would not have to rob them. In contrast, the super-apostles used their wealth as proof of God's blessing.

> THE DEVIL LONGS TO BE AN ALTERNATE SOURCE OF ILLUMINATION AND INTERPRETATION.

I've been told that one of the most famous "prophets," or evangelists, claims that the dead will soon be raised in his crusades. But if a person does not preach "Jesus Christ and him crucified" (1 Corinthians 2:2), and if the Cross is not the center of his ministry, and if he makes promises to his followers that God has not actually made, I agree with Jim Cymbala, who says that he would not follow such a person, *even if he is able to raise the dead!*

Without an understanding of the Cross; without teaching that we can be saved only through the sacrifice of Christ, it matters not that the preacher's predictions come to pass. At the end of the day, we know that a preacher is from God, not because he can predict the future, not because he can do miracles, but because he preaches "Christ and him crucified." Any deviation from this is "another gospel."

What question did I ask Phil (referred to earlier) that led me to believe that the prophet/priest who made an accurate prediction was not of God? I asked, "How would this man answer this question: What does a person have to do to enter heaven?" Phil answered, "He would say that you have to follow God and be a good person." That, of course is "another gospel," proof that even prophets with right predictions are not necessarily sent by God.

They Have Their Own Source of Power

We continue. "For such men are false apostles, deceitful workmen, masquerading as apostles of Christ. And no wonder, for Satan himself masquerades as an angel of light. It is not surprising, then, if his servants masquerade as servants of righteousness. Their end will be what their actions deserve" (2 Corinthians 11:13–15). Keep in mind that Satan's most delightful deception is to pretend to be the Holy Spirit. His goal is to reveal knowledge that cannot be known through the Scriptures or reason. Some of what he reveals may be true; some of it is false. If he needs to mix his error with truth in order to deceive, he will do so.

His most dazzling deception is to give revelations to those who are available to receive them. This is why Paul said, "But I am afraid that just as Eve was deceived by the serpent's cunning, your minds may somehow be led astray from your sincere and pure devotion to Christ" (v. 3). The serpent deceived Eve by giving her a revelation that seemed to supersede the Word of God. God had spoken, but she was now given further insight that God had denied her. Thus today we have the "God told me" preachers who keep claiming additional light and further knowledge. Some of these "revelations" are consistent with the Word of God; others are fantastic tales and bizarre insights. The devil longs to be an alternate source of illumination and interpretation.

If Satan had been interviewed on a television program two thousand years ago, we can almost hear him say, "I just received a new revelation from God! The Lord has just told me that based on Psalm 91:11–12, we can jump from the pinnacle of the temple and not get hurt! Praise God!" False prophets frequently find a verse, often wrested from its context, to make some  "new" interpretation, intended to impress their hearers. Ignorant of principles of interpretation, and equally unacquainted with the wisdom of past teachers of the church, these prophets are free to put whatever words they wish in the mouth of God.

Listen to the teachings of those who belong to the Word of Faith Movement, and you will hear occultism mixed with Scripture taken out of context. You will hear that the power to create reality lies within yourself; all that is needed is faith that one's word is imbued with magical powers. Creative visualization is needed to have faith in one's own faith. This, of course, is the teaching of occult groups such as the Science of Mind and the New Age Movement.[3]

People are told that they can speak to their wallets and say, "Wallet, by my faith you will be filled with money." Or they can speak to their bodies and say, "Body, you are just wonderful, healthy, and good." This kind of magic-speak is taught to millions, who accept it as if it were from the Bible. Satan's prophets masquerading as prophets, not of deceit but of *righteousness!*

Second, this demonic power is seen in miracles, often

miracles beyond those found in the Scriptures. One evangelist claimed that he would do miracles "geater than these in
the book of Acts." If you were the devil, how could you better deceive people than to do a miracle that was of physical
or material benefit but detracted from the work of Jesus on
the cross? Deception is often subtle.

Ted Brooks, a pastor of a church that emphasized miracles, tongues, and prophecies, but who has since seen the
errors of his teaching, wrote:

> Just because words spoken by Christian leaders sound
> spiritual doesn't mean that they should be heeded. The
> spirits of Antichrist within the Church will confess many
> spiritual things. They will even quote much of the Bible.
> They will perform signs and wonders, which fascinate
> the soul. They will appear as apostles, prophets, and pas-
> tors, but they will avoid pointing us to the fact that Jesus
> Christ was the complete revelation of God's will and
> character in the flesh.[4]

He goes on to say that when you examine these miracles
you are called a miracle hater or a man of unbelief. But we
cannot be intimidated. A true miracle will not fall apart if it is
carefully examined. False miracle workers believe that if they
do something that not even Jesus or the apostles did, this
proves they are of God. Thus people are "slain in the spirit"
and sometimes uncontrollable laughter overtakes a congregation. Indeed, the more bizarre the happening, the more
likely it is thought to be of God. To quote Brooks again, "The
never-been-done-before is a sign of a true miracle of God."[5]

Some tell their congregations to put their Bibles away and enter into all that God is doing.

Sound biblical interpretation is thrown aside in favor of the "new thing" God is doing. If a man gets down on his hands and knees and roars like a lion, they will say it is scriptural because the Bible in various places mentions lions. If a man speaks gibberish, whatever interpretation given is accepted, even if the revelation did not come in a human language as happened in the book of Acts. Everything is assumed to be manifestations from God.

The contemporary phenomenon of being "slain in the spirit" is not only absent in Scripture, it is contrary to the kinds of ministries done by Christ and the apostles. Again, we quote Peter Fenwick, a charismatic who has much in sympathy with the manifestation of gifts. He says that he personally knows many, both before and after the experience of "being slain in the spirit."

Fenwick writes: "Many . . . report pleasant experiences of 'carpet time' but I detect no fundamental changes of the sort that are being claimed. To me, of course, this comes as no surprise, in view of the general absence of the Word of God within the Toronto Blessing."[6] This fits the spirit of the age: Just as people want to hear from God without the difficult work of studying the Bible, so they want to have spiritual maturity without the difficult work of prayer, Bible study, learning to witness, and the like.

But are there not instances of people being "slain in the spirit" in past revivals? Accounts that have come down to us from the days of Jonathan Edwards and John Wesley are often used to justify the present phenomena seen so often on television. Yes, there are reports of "manifestations" of various kinds, but keep in mind that (1) many who "fell" did so under deep conviction of sin and (2) the revivalists not only discouraged the practice, but believed that these occurrences often detracted from the gospel message itself. And (3) these manifestations did not happen because people were touched by an evangelist who gave them a jolt of spiritual power. Finally, (4) never were these manifestations put on public display to encourage others to have the same experience.

Today's super-apostles claim to do in a matter of minutes what older preachers told us could only come about by daily brokenness and submission to God, usually through suffering. Today we are told we can have power just by being touched by a super-charged apostle.

Yes, they have their own power.

They Have Their Own Means of Control

Paul chides the Corinthian believers, "In fact, you even put up with anyone who enslaves you or exploits you or takes advantage of you or pushes himself forward or *slaps you in the face*" (2 Corinthians 11:20, emphasis added). Imagine! These believers were willing to be mistreated by these super-apostles without complaint! These false teachers were manipulative, controlling, and demeaning, and the gullible people followed them!

Human nature has not changed! I marvel at the stories I hear about people attending churches where the pastor uses his authority to exploit the people through arrogant control, belittling comments, and accusations. In some instances, the pastor will threaten church members, even so far as cursing them, should they leave his congregation. He demands absolute loyalty, commitment, and personal obedience. The people continue to attend, though he "slaps them in the face," as Paul put it. After all, the pastor claims to be God's special servant.

How do false prophets exercise such control?

First, through isolation. Often they will cut their followers off from their families, insisting that their loyalty be to the false teachers alone. They will insist that their members communicate only with them; after all, the prophet will tell them all they need to know. This, of course, is often the mark of a false cult.

Second, there is intimidation. If false prophets get to know you personally, they will find some weakness in your life and then use this as a lever to bribe you into subjection. One false teacher asked those in his small groups about their sexual fantasies and later used this information against them. About twenty years ago, one false prophet here in the Chicago area told me that if I did not come under his authority, he already saw me "falling." That can be intimidating if you think he actually speaks on God's behalf.

> A FALSE PROPHET WILL USUALLY DRAW ATTENTION TO HIMSELF.

Third, there is exploitation. Again, the false teacher finds ways to develop connections with his clientele. If he is a media personality, he assures them of a special favor if they write to him. He promises answers to their prayers; he promises prosperity; he promises that God will reward them with money. He craves cultic dependency and trust. Then he can depend on their loyalty and support for years to come.

Meanwhile, false prophets will not themselves be under

authority. They will challenge the authority of the elders, or they will pick board members whom they know will not hold them accountable. Since they believe they get their orders directly from God, when they are questioned, they will retort, "Who are you to question the Lord's anointed?"

If a miracle happens in their ministry, they parade it in front of the crowds and, by implication, get the credit as a "miracle worker." But if someone is not healed, it is the fault of the person who didn't have enough faith or didn't give enough money, and so on. No one is ever called to the platform to testify of his "non-healing."

Have you noticed that the crowds that come to admire the miracle workers are often the poor? Because these people —bless them—are thinking, *If I could have as much faith as my leader, God would bless me like God has blessed him.* So if they do not have their mortgage paid automatically; if they do not experience healing, then it is their own fault. No wonder I have had disillusioned people from these ministries tell me they believe that God has forsaken them.

They Have Their Own Means of Self-Exaltation

A false prophet will usually draw attention to himself. Like Diotrephes, they want to have the preeminence (3 John 9). Peter gives this vivid description: "For they mouth empty, boastful words and, by appealing to the lustful desires of sinful human nature, they entice people who are just escaping from those who live in error" (2 Peter 2:18). Some mouth empty boasts by having the audacity to give commands to God, telling Him what to do. On television I saw an evangelist say to a woman who had been unable to bear children:

"What do you want, a boy or a girl?"

"A boy."

"It will be a boy. What color eyes?"

"Blue eyes."

"He will have blue eyes. When do you want him to be born?"

"Next year."

"He will be born next year!"

Then he went on to say that if she had chosen twins, she would have had twins! Imagine!

What will happen, however, if this couple does not have a

> ARE WE WILLING TO FOLLOW A CHRIST WHO HAS TAUGHT US TO SUFFER WELL?

blue-eyed boy, born next year? What if they have a brown-eyed girl, born the following year? Or what if they continue to have no children at all? Will they say, "We were duped by a false prophet!"? No, more probably they will say, "If only we had had more faith, God would have fulfilled His word to us." In the minds of devoted followers, the so-called prophet always wins; only the common people lose.

Some prophets will draw attention to themselves by their own appearance. In the early days of the church, Appolonius wrote a document about false prophets in which he said that they could be recognized by their dress and demeanor. "Tell me, does a prophet dye his hair? Does a prophet use stibium [a bright, silvery, crystalline substance] on his eyes? Is a prophet fond of dress?"[7] False prophets, he contended, like to be the center of attention. All of us have to keep in mind that it is not possible for us to exalt ourselves and exalt Christ simultaneously.

Billy Graham is proof that fame need not corrupt and

that genuine humility can exist in a man who is admired by millions. His commitment to the centrality of the gospel is a model for us all.

PAUL'S FAILURE TO MEASURE UP

How did Paul look in contrast to these "super-apostles"? The answer is weak and pitiful. "To my shame I admit that we were too weak for that!" (2 Corinthians 11:21). He was too "weak" to use the techniques of the false prophets. They made him look weak because he was unattractive and unable to preach as well as they; what is more, his physical presence was unimpressive. One early report says that Paul was short, bald-headed, and bowlegged. Imagine the ratings if he were on television!

Can't you just hear it already? "Paul just doesn't have what these other leaders do. . . . We want teachers who have enough faith that God will pay off our loans; the ones who don't have to suffer. We want someone who has the power to rebuke a thorn in the flesh rather than live with it victoriously!" And so while Paul was willing to continue to suffer for the sake of the Cross, these teachers were offering an easier, alternative path.

Interestingly, in the rest of 2 Corinthians 11, Paul goes on to argue that his badge of authority was not his ability to do miracles but the suffering he endured (vv. 21–33)! He says, in effect, "You know that I am a true apostle because God has given me the grace to suffer so well." He was flogged five times, beaten with rods three times, and stoned and shipwrecked. All this, and more, is what gave his ministry credibility.

The people at Corinth had to make a choice: Did they want to be like Paul, who had no money and suffered, or did they want to be like the false prophets with their fancy clothes? Today we would say, "Do we want to be followers of false prophets with their gold chains, Rolex watches, and fancy cars? Or are we willing to follow a Christ who has taught us to suffer well." As did the believers in Corinth, we have a choice to make.

Paul's message and authority came from God; those of his detractors came from Satan. He argued that the marks of a true prophet are suffering and hardship, not health and wealth. Even Jesus did not change the world through miracles but through His suffering.

And so it has ever been.

NOTES

1. Scott Hafeman, comment made in a telephone call to the author, October 2001.
2. K. Neil Foster, *Sorting Out the Supernatural* (Camp Hill, Pa.: Christian Publications, 2001), 245.
3. Hank Hanegraaff, *Christianity in Crisis* (Eugene, Oreg.: Harvest, 1993), 82–83.
4. Ted Brooks, *I Was a Flaky Preacher* (Belleville, Ontario: Guardian, 1999), 38.
5. Ibid., 43.
6. Peter Fenwick, in Clifford Hill, Peter Fenwick, David Forbes, and David Noakes, *Blessing the Church?* (Guildford, Surrey [U.K.]: Eagle, 1995), 60.
7. Foster, *Sorting Out the Supernatural,* 22.

WHEN YOU JUDGE MIRACLES

Are They from God or the Devil?

O ur culture is awash with miracles.

When Oprah Winfrey's movie *Beloved* was released, she reported that she had "channeled" some of the historical characters that appeared in the film. In an interview she said that "old spirits" were trying "to get in touch with her." She said that she heard the voices of slaves—they even have names—and "has come to know each of them personally and calls them in at will" to guide her in her work. Before the various scenes were filmed, she spent time burning candles and channeling the spirits of the past. "She would literally channel the spirit of Margaret Garner, the inspiration for Sethe [the slave] into her performance," said Jonathan Demme, who worked with Oprah on the set.[1]

Yes, mysticism, with its attendant spirituality, is attractive, and millions are trying to connect with the metaphysical realm (that is, the spiritual aspect of the universe). It is a world filled with self-realization, spirit guides, and, yes, a world of miracles.

In local libraries, shelves are stacked with books on miracles, telling dozens of stories:

- A phantom dog appears out of the fog to guide a family away from danger.
- A silent hitchhiker leads a doctor to a school bus crash.
- A guardian angel gets a sick child to a hospital.
- A trucker saves a life after hearing a call for help over his CB radio—but no call was ever sent.

I also have read sections of a book titled *A Course in Miracles,* written by Helen Schuchman. Where did she get her information on how to perform miracles? She was introduced to a voice that told her everything she needed to know. "It made no sound, but seemed to be giving me a kind of rapid, inner dictation which I took down in a shorthand notebook. . . . It made me very uncomfortable, but it never seriously occurred to me to stop. It seemed to be a special assignment I had somehow, somewhere agreed to complete."[2]

> A MIRACLE IS NOT NECESSARILY FROM GOD JUST BECAUSE IT HELPS PEOPLE.

This primer is replete with references to God, the Holy Spirit, and even occasional references to Christ. The premises of the book have much in common with Eastern mysticism: We share our lives with God, human nature is fundamentally good, and miracles are waiting to happen if we just recognize the fact that we have the power to perform them. Death is a dream, there is no judgment, and salvation is entering into the freedom that awaits anyone who has faith in himself. In such a world, miracles are common.

Recently, a national television program carried the story of a girl lying in a coma but believed to be a saint. Proof of this is that a statue of the Virgin Mary begot tears when the young woman was brought home from the hospital. Other religious objects have also begun to weep, and oil appears in vases left where a small shrine has been established. Many people are coming to look at the sick child, requesting that she pray for them. If possible, visitors leave with a drop of the holy oil. Some say they have been healed.

PRELIMINARY WARNINGS

Jesus had much to say about miracles:

"Not everyone who says to me, 'Lord, Lord,' will enter the kingdom of heaven, but only he who does the will of my Father who is in heaven. Many will say to me on that day, 'Lord, Lord, did we not prophesy in your name, and in your name drive out demons and perform many miracles?' Then I will tell them plainly, 'I never knew you. Away from me, you evildoers!'" (Matthew 7:21–23)

Jesus gives us three warnings. First, a miracle is not necessarily from God just because it is performed by one who calls Jesus "Lord." There are miracle workers who speak respectfully of Christ; they acknowledge that, indeed, He is the Lord; and yet these miracle workers are not sent by God. In order to know that a miracle is from God, it has to be based on sound doctrine; but note that even sound doctrine is no absolute proof that a miracle is from God.

Second, a miracle is not necessarily from God just because it helps people. In this text, Jesus assures us that demons were evidently cast out and beneficial miracles were performed. Yet, the miracles did not originate in the power of God.

Third, we have often wondered: Do false prophets and miracle workers know that they are deceived? Some, perhaps, know that they are fakes, deliberately exploiting the people. But others are sincere, believing their miraculous gifts to be from God. This is why Jesus gives us a third warning: A miracle is not necessarily of God just because the miracle worker seems to have assurance of heaven.

> THE PRIMARY PURPOSE OF THE MIRACLES WAS TO AUTHENTICATE THE MESSAGE OF CHRIST AND THE APOSTLES.

Notice that these people were expecting to be within the pearly gates! They were surprised and horrified at being "turned away." They preached a Christ and called Him Lord, and yet they were not converted! We can be quite sure that these miracles were done by people who spoke endlessly about heaven, eternal life, and the like. In fact, maybe these are the people who told us we did not have to wait for heaven but could have it all now.

But are there false prophets who are also genuine Christians? Others may disagree, but I believe the answer is yes. In my judgment, some who are saved are nonetheless deceived about their own ability to "hear from the Lord." Others have miraculous powers they have never tested but simply assume to be from God. If you are taught that every

healing is from God, then it is easy to see why genuine believers are often drawn into false teaching and false miracles. This explains why the same mouth that utters foolish
revelations can at times give authentic biblical teaching. It
might also explain why the same man who can "slay in the
spirit" can later turn around and tell people that they need
to believe on Christ to be saved.

If we ask why God allows such a mixture of the false
and the true to exist together—even perhaps in the same
person—we can only answer that He does this to test us.
This, you might recall, is the reason God gave the Israelites
as to why He might allow a false prophet to mouth an accurate prophecy. "The LORD your God is *testing* you to find out
whether you love him with all your heart and with all your
soul" (Deuteronomy 13:3, emphasis added).

A BRIEF HISTORY OF MIRACLES

Miracles appear on every page of the New Testament.
"When our Lord came down to earth He drew heaven with
Him," wrote B. B. Warfield in his classic book *Counterfeit
Miracles*.[3] He argues that Christ's countless miracles—which
might number in the hundreds—were never intended to
continue on through the church age. Certainly the apostles
also performed miraculous signs, but after their time, miracles disappeared from Christendom. Disappeared, that is,
until a few centuries later when they "reappeared" as bor-
rowed superstitions. Pagan folklore, replete with stories of
miracles, was recounted in the Christian church.

When Christianity came to Rome, it entered a culture
that was already rife with what might be called the cult of

spirituality. Belief in the Roman gods meant belief in miraculous powers. Indeed, the primary purpose of the gods, as the pagans saw it, was to benefit human beings. Warfield says that "men floated in a world of miracles like a fish in water."[4] The more miraculous a story, the more it was believed. The whole population of the Roman Empire was caught in a "gigantic net of superstition."

Interestingly, there are reports of the dead being raised among the heathen. In an age when medical knowledge was limited, and superstitions abounded, there were those who were thought to be dead and then resuscitated. If Christians had pointed to miracles to attest their message, the heathen world would have been unimpressed; they claimed their miracles, too; even fantastic accounts of the raising of the dead.

Rather than shunning these miracle stories, the Christian church actually embraced them (albeit with interpretive license) and made them a part of Christian folklore. The name of Jesus was substituted for the name of a pagan god. Thus, in the name of Jesus, bolts on doors sprang open, idols were overturned, poisons were rendered harmless, the sick were healed, and the dead were raised.[5] In a superstitious age, these stories were accepted as part of the miracle workings of Christianity. The pagan accounts of miracles were dependent on hearsay, fragmentary descriptions, and popular folklore. Sadly, Christians accepted these stories, retelling them within a Christian context.

The simple fact is this: The primary purpose of the miracles was to authenticate the message of Christ and the apostles. Christ continually linked His claims to His works, proving that His intention was not to heal as many people as possible but to do a variety of miracles that would convince His disciples and spiritually-minded onlookers that He was indeed the Christ. The apostles likewise did miracles, bestowing the gift of the Holy Spirit and, in some instances, empowering others by the laying on of hands. But as that generation died out, the miraculous powers, for the most part, died out with them.

Can it be shown that the Scriptures themselves teach that the apostolic age was one of miracles, not necessarily intended to continue throughout the history of the church? I think so. Paul spoke of the signs of an apostle, "The things that mark an apostle—signs, wonders and miracles—were done among you with great perseverance" (2 Corinthians 12:12). Yes, the apostles did have the authority to do such miracles, but there is no compelling evidence that these would continue.

The author of Hebrews echoes the same connection between the newly revealed message of God and the miraculous signs. "This salvation, which was first announced by the Lord, was confirmed to us by those who heard him. God also testified to it by signs, wonders and various miracles, and gifts of the Holy Spirit distributed according to his will (Hebrews 2:3–4). The miracles confirmed the message; the miracles were testimony that a new revelation had come from God. There is reason to believe that Warfield was right when he said, "Their abundant display in the Apostolic Church is the mark of the richness of the apostolic age in revelation; and when this revelation period closed, the period for the miracle-working had passed."[6] God gave us His revelation at one time in an organic whole, and when that was closed, the age of miracles, for the most part, was closed along with it. As John Calvin said, "It is unreasonable to ask for miracles—or to find them—where there is no new gospel."

Of course not all signs and wonders today are either fake, of the devil, or otherwise unbiblical. Certainly there are some accounts today of healings, miraculous "coincidences," and other such happenings, usually in answer to the prayers of God's people. Unfortunately, there are also spurious miracles that mislead and deceive. My plea here is for the need of discernment and the realization that not all miraculous occurrences are from God. Nor do we have the right to expect a repeat of the many miracles recorded on the pages of the New Testament.

> CHRISTIANITY IS NOT UNIQUE BECAUSE OF ITS MIRACLES.

Jesus warned, "For false Christs and false prophets will appear and perform great signs and miracles to deceive even the elect—if that were possible" (Matthew 24:24). In other words, we cannot be too careful when we judge miracles. We could be deceived either way: We could ascribe the works of the devil to God, and we also stand in danger of ascribing the works of God to the devil. Christ's point is that the false is so much like the true that it is almost impossible to tell the difference.

SEPARATING THE FALSE FROM THE TRUE

Christianity is a supernatural religion. I agree with the missionary statesman Hudson Taylor, who said, "We are a supernatural people born again by a supernatural birth, kept by a supernatural Teacher from a supernatural Book.

We are led by a supernatural Captain in right paths and assured victories."[7] But the nature of that supernaturalism must be judged by the Scriptures themselves. Since there are many miracles performed by the "other side" of the supernatural world, we must take note of the warnings of Scripture and try to discern the true from the false.

Here are some principles I hope will be of help.

The Gospel vs. Miracles

The power of Christianity is best seen in the gospel, not in physical miracles. Paul wrote, "Jews demand miraculous signs and Greeks look for wisdom, but we preach Christ crucified: a stumbling block to Jews and foolishness to Gentiles, but to those whom God has called, both Jews and Greeks, Christ the power of God and the wisdom of God" (1 Corinthians 1:22–24).

Some people teach that we could evangelize more effectively if we had signs and wonders to authenticate the gospel message. In fact, the Vineyard Movement, begun in the 1970s, teaches that our churches should be characterized by healings, along with "words of knowledge" and speaking in tongues. In the previous chapter we spoke about those who are "slain in the spirit," falling down in the presence of TV preachers, supposedly under the power of the Holy Spirit. There are also reports of angelic visitations, predictions made about coming revivals, and personal stories claiming virtually any "miracle" one can imagine.

However, many of these signs and wonders are more in keeping with the hyper-spirituality of popular culture than the teachings of the Bible. For example, Peter Wagner gives five steps to be followed in obtaining the miracle of healing. In the fourth stage, he says, "Sometimes there is a fluttering of the eyelids or a kind of aura that surrounds the person. Sometimes there are other manifestations."[8] One writer says that, when this gift is conferred, there is a change in color of the evangelist's hands that proves "you've got some intercession that's gone up that Papa's saying yes to. . . . Because when my hands turn purple it means you're getting through to Royalty; you're getting through to the top."[9]

Evangelists are encouraged to follow the lead of those who "taunt the spirits" in an anticipation of an evening of power. The late John Wimber, who founded the Vineyard Movement, said that the two most important miracles for impressing unbelievers are "falling in the power of the Spirit and filling teeth."[10] Some of the Vineyard prophets actually claim to "smell God" when those seeking healing come to them as the walls of their offices dissolve and they see visions of the person's past. Clouds with dollar signs appear over the heads of people in an auditorium who have financial problems. John Armstrong is quite correct when he writes, "Advance courses in healing are offered, as though it were training in the magical arts."[11]

> MIRACLES MUST NEVER DETRACT FROM OUR RESPONSIBILITY TO SHOWCASE THE GOSPEL OF THE CROSS.

Such an approach blends nicely with the superstition, magic, and spiritual dimensions of the New Age Movement. No wonder Wimber actually defended the practice of employing medieval relics in healing. "In the Catholic Church for over a 1,200-year period people were healed as a result of touching the relics of the saints. We Protestants have difficulty with that . . . but we healers shouldn't, because there is nothing theologically out of line with that."[12]

However, we must remember that Christianity is not unique because of its miracles. Alan Cole, who has served Christ in many different cultures, writes of the Vineyard Movement:

> None of these signs are new to me (healings, visions, tongues, exorcisms). But the trouble is that I have seen *every one of them* (yes, tongues too) in non-Christian religions, and outwardly there was no difference in the signs, except that one was done in the name of Jesus and the other was not. Of course, if the person was also responding to the Gospel, there was real and lasting change in life. That is why I cannot get excited about healings in themselves, and why I can reverently understand how Jesus used them sparingly, and retreated when the crowds became too great.[13]

Keep in mind that "testimonies of healing appear in every issue of the *Christian Science Sentinel*. Pakistani Muslims claim that one of their revered saints, Baba Farid, has healed people with incurable diseases. Thousands of Hindus claim healing each year at the temple dedicated to Venkateswara in Tirupathi."[14]

Do we need miracles to authenticate the gospel?

After Luther published his Ninety-five Theses and the Reformation movement was underway, the Catholic Church argued that it had statues that would cry and relics that multiplied themselves (thus the explanation for the hundreds of pieces of wood that were supposed to have come from the cross of Christ). Furthermore, Rome argued that it had recorded apparitions of Mary and Christ. Miraculous healings took place when the worshipers touched the relics of the saints. "Where are your miracles?" the church taunted the Reformers.

The Reformers insisted that the gospel had its own power. Paul wrote, "I am not ashamed of the gospel, *because it is the power of God for the salvation of everyone who believes:* first for the Jew, then for the Gentile" (Romans 1:16, emphasis added). As quoted above, when Paul came to Corinth, he chided the people who sought signs; and as for himself, he emphasized "Christ the power of God and the wisdom of God" (1 Corinthians 1:24).

> THE MORE MIRACLES JESUS PERFORMED, THE MORE OPPOSITION TOWARD HIM GREW.

Interestingly, no church in the New Testament is judged for not doing more signs and wonders. But Paul rebuked churches for an unclear gospel (Galatians) and an overemphasis on gifts along with a worldly spirit (Corinth) and the dangers of accepting a Gnostic view of Christ (Colossians). Christ's rebukes to the seven churches were either doctrinal, moral, or both. Never once did He hint that they needed more signs and wonders.

Of course we must emphasize that God may do miracles, and does do miracles, but it is unwise to focus on them rather than the gospel message. Miracles must never detract from our responsibility to showcase the gospel of the Cross.

Miracles as Redemptive Acts of God

"But"—we can already hear the question—"were there not plenty of signs and wonders in the Bible? Why should we think God has limited Himself in this age?" As one person said to me, "If God is the same from age to age, why would His works not continue to our times?"

These are fair questions. So I would like to begin by saying that, yes, there might be signs and wonders today, for we have no right to limit God. But our first obligation is to find out the biblical purpose of these phenomena and then to judge contemporary claims by this standard. In the Bible, signs and wonders are redemptive acts of God. "He sent his signs and wonders into your midst, O Egypt, against Pharaoh and all his servants" (Psalm 135:9). Thus we should not be surprised that the New Testament applies the expression to the ministry of Christ (Acts 2:22; see also 2:19; 4:30; 5:12). John calls the miracles of Christ *signs,* which were to lead people to believe that Jesus was the Christ (John 20:30–31).

However, and this is important, not all signs and wonders in the Bible are attributed to the gracious acts of God. "The Egyptian magicians could match Moses miracle for miracle," turning the Nile into blood, producing frogs, and the like.[15] Not until the magicians were expected to bring forth gnats were they forced to admit failure (Exodus 8:18). Interestingly, these "false wonders" are not interpreted for us in Scripture. We are not told if these magicians did their miracles by sleight of hand or by the power of the devil. All that we know is that these soothsayers "did the same" miracles as Moses.

Even the signs and wonders recorded in Scripture were insufficient to persuade the unconverted to believe in Christ. The more miracles Jesus performed, the more opposition toward Him grew. On the day of Pentecost, Peter said that

Christ was "accredited by God to you by miracles . . . and signs" (Acts 2:22), yet most in the crowd were not brought to faith until they heard the gospel through Peter's lips.

Perhaps we could summarize it this way: Miracles attested to the person of Christ for those who were open to the truth; even those who had their doubts (as did Thomas) were reassured by the miraculous. But the skeptics either denied the miracles or ascribed them to the devil. This best explains why Jesus performed miracles so that some would believe but, on the other hand, refused to do miracles for the truly skeptical. Even today there is no compelling evidence that when the unconverted see miracles they are more disposed to believe the gospel.

Again, I must stress that I am not saying that authentic signs and wonders *cannot* occur today or even that they *do not* occur today. There is no hard scriptural evidence that the gift of miracles has been rescinded. What we do know is that such miracles are of lesser importance than a clear gospel witness and the quest for holiness. Yes, we can believe God today for miracles, but we cannot demand them; and we should not be led to expect them on a regular basis. And we most assuredly cannot subcribe to the modern notion that they are needed to do effective evangelism in a culture already saturated with bogus miracles of every sort.

We can do no better than quote the words of Jesus:

"A wicked and adulterous generation asks for a miraculous sign! But none will be given it except the sign of the prophet Jonah. For as Jonah was three days and three nights in the belly of a huge fish, so the Son of Man will be three days and three nights in the heart of the earth."
(Matthew 12:39–40)

Today multitudes thirst for signs but will not believe the powerful evidence for the death and resurrection of Christ.

No Promises for Instant Healing

There is no promise that we can have a miracle (such as healing) if we just have the faith to receive it. The fact that Jesus healed so many people has led some to conclude that divine healing is the prerogative of every Christian. Some faith healers teach that it is God's will for every Christian to be healed, at all times.

The theology of many faith healers assumes that all sickness is of the devil, Christ came to defeat Satan, and thus we can be healed whenever we meet the conditions. Entailed within these assumptions is the cruel notion that if you are not healed, it is your fault: a lack of faith, a lack of appropriating the promises, and in some cases, a lack of seeking the gift of tongues.

We cannot calculate the widespread devastation this false teaching has brought to tens of thousands of sincere believers who sought healing and did not find it. "God has forsaken me!" a woman wept as she told me that she believed that healing was hers to have, but because of her lack of faith she was rejected by God. She represents the countless souls who have accepted this theology not knowing that it is seriously flawed.

Paul was not healed from his "thorn in the flesh" and came to understand that this affliction (possibly malaria) was God's will for him (see 2 Corinthians 12:7–10).

Yes, there are times in the Gospels when Jesus puts responsibility for the absence of miracles on the people who refused to believe (Matthew 13:58). But on a personal level, Jesus never tried to heal a person only to turn away because he or she did not have enough faith. Indeed, He often healed people sovereignly without demanding any faith at all. There does not seem to be a clear pattern in Jesus' healing ministry.

The best-known promise for divine healing is found in Isaiah 53, where we are told that "by his wounds we are healed" (v. 5). Jesus went about healing people so that these words were fulfilled: "He took up our infirmities and carried our diseases" (Matthew 8:17). Peter wrote, "He Himself bore our sins in His body on the cross, that we might die to sin and live to righteousness; for by His wounds you were healed" (1 Peter 2:24 NASB).

Some theologians who are skeptical of divine healing have labored to prove that the healing spoken of in these passages is spiritual, not physical. But the context in Matthew and the implication of Peter is that Christ did indeed die for our physical bodies. In fact, it is consistent with Scripture to affirm that Christ came to redeem the whole man—body, soul, and spirit.

But does this mean that we can have physical healing whenever we prayerfully meet the conditions? Clearly the answer is no. Although Christ died for our bodies as well as our souls, we will not see the fulfillment of that aspect of our redemption until we are resurrected into glory. Christ came to redeem us from sin, but we still have a sin nature; He came to destroy death, yet we die; He came to redeem our bodies, yet we are subject to accidents, poisons, and the frailty of the flesh. Our resurrected body was purchased by Christ, but today the body we carefully nurture is subject to disease. Yes, of course, some day the enemy death will be taken away, but we aren't there yet.

We must humbly admit that there are no promises that say we can be healed whenever we wish if only we had the faith. If there were, we would not have to die until the Lord returns. We could just keep claiming our healing again and again. You should not be surprised that there are people today who think that an endless life is indeed possible, based on divine promises. I knew a man, who has since died, who believed that

> PRAYER ENABLED CHRIST TO GATHER STRENGTH TO GO THROUGH WITH HIS ASSIGNMENT; IT WAS NOT THE MEANS OF DELIVERING HIM FROM IT.

he would live until the Lord returned. But even the faith healer, whom he most admired, is now dead.

Many who teach that divine healing is instantly available wear glasses, get arthritis, and have implanted hearing aids. All these infirmities bear eloquent testimony to the fact that in this life we see only the beginning of redemption. Yes, sometimes God does heal (particularly as seen in the ministry of Christ), but even then the healing is merely a postponement of future illness and death. Even Christ's healings on earth were not permanent. The people He healed, died.

This misunderstanding of the promises of Scripture has been the source of much grief in the Christian community. People who claim healing, insisting that God is obligated to keep His promises, often end up feeling betrayed. When healing does not occur, they point to these verses and say that God cannot be trusted. Or they try to find some other reason, such as unbelief or unconfessed sin, to explain why they were not healed. Since they believe they have heard God correctly, they take the fault upon themselves to protect His reputation.

A charismatic writer admitted that unbiblical theology about healing creates heartache and confusion. He wrote:

> Bad theology is a cruel taskmaster . . . shepherds have to bind up the wounds after the traveling teachers and evangelists are gone and the ravaged sheep are left behind. We cannot therefore, do without an adequate Biblical theology of healing. We need a theology that squarely faces facts; I often tell my students, "If your theology doesn't fit the facts, change your theology." Jesus is not, after all, a Christian Scientist.[16]

Yes, bad theology is a cruel taskmaster.

The closest Christ ever came to using a prayer as the means to escape physical and spiritual distress was when He prayed in Gethsemane: "Abba! Father! All things are possible for You; remove this cup from Me; yet not what I will, but what You will" (Mark 14:36 NASB).

Christ had every right to ask the Father for anything; why did He not insist that He be exempted from the impending torture of the cross? That answer is that *it was God's will that Christ suffer*. The prayer of Gethsemane was the means that Christ used to receive the grace and power to do the will of God. Prayer enabled Christ to gather strength to go through with His assignment; it was not the means of delivering Him from it.

We see no evidence in the New Testament that some people began a healing ministry, dispensing healing to those who would come to them. On occasion, Peter and Paul healed the sick, but it was incidental to their evangelistic/ discipleship ministry. First and foremost, they were known not as healers but as evangelists, engaging men and women in dialogue about the Messiah.

Let us keep in mind that God *sometimes* heals the body but *always* heals the souls of those who come to Him in humility and faith. "He heals the brokenhearted and binds up their wounds" (Psalm 147:3). To keep our priorities biblical is always our greatest challenge.

We can be grateful that the charismatic movement has challenged all of us to expect greater things from God. But we dare not elevate the so-called supernatural gifts above the quest for personal holiness, evangelism, and single-minded discipleship.

I have often wished that faith healers would look into the television cameras and say to their audience, *It is better to be holy than to be healed.*

Miracles Benefit God's People

God is gracious in giving rain and sunshine to the just as well as the unjust. In that sense, He blesses the whole world. But there are also special acts of providence, those special times of intervention that God does on behalf of His people.

To invite people to be healed or receive a miracle without knowing what they believe about Christ or what their lifestyle is seems out of character with the teaching of the Bible. I attended a healing service by a faith healer who supposedly was used by God to perform miracles. I say *supposedly,* because I was close enough to the platform to ask those who "claimed healing" about their experience, and in later discussions, I learned that many did not actually experience a miracle, despite the claims of the healer.

However, what interested me was one man who supposedly was healed of deafness. He came to the platform to "claim" his hearing, and the evangelist "tested" the man's hearing ability and thousands clapped, rejoicing in the miracle. But as the healed man left the platform, the evangelist asked, "By the way, are you a Christian?" and he replied, "No, I am a Muslim." He was asked to return to the platform for special prayer.

Obviously, God can, if He wishes, heal someone from whatever religion, but I do not find such examples in the Scripture. Miracles were not done indiscriminately, no matter what people believed or what God they served. That is not to say that everyone Jesus healed already believed in Him as the Son of God; but so far as I know they did end up believing in Him after the miracle was performed.

That is why I believe that the gifts of healing in the New Testament were to be exercised within the context of the local church. Thus, those who needed healing would be known to the leadership, who could ascertain the spiritual commitment and lifestyle of those who were prayed for. The apostles could do miracles in the vicinity of Jerusalem because there were many people who had believed that Jesus was the Messiah. But nowhere in the epistles do we have mention of healing services where people were invited to be healed without regard for their religion and lifestyle. This was simply foreign to the New Testament.

Usually we use the phrase "gift of healing," but three

times the apostle Paul used the plural "gifts of healings" to speak about a special endowment of miraculous powers (1 Corinthians 12:9, 28, 30). This use of the plural strongly suggests that there were different gifts of healings. Perhaps, as D. A. Carson suggests, not everyone was getting healed by one person, and perhaps certain persons with one of these gifts could heal certain diseases or heal a variety of diseases at certain times. Thus, even if someone were to be healed by the gifts of one person at a particular time, that would not mean that a "gift of healing" had been bestowed upon the individual and that he or she should enter a full-time healing ministry.[17] Interestingly, Paul, who exercised the gift of healing, left Trophimus sick at Miletus (2 Timothy 4:20). Evidently even his gift could not be used in every situation.

I shall not argue, as some have, that these gifts passed off the scene with the death of the apostles, although we have already shown that there was a precipitous decline in miracles by the second century. We would agree that Christ, who is the Lord of the church, is able to bestow such gifts according to His will even today.

But clearly these gifts were to be exercised by the people of God in behalf of the people of God. There is no hint that these gifts and the blessings that accompany them were for those who believed in whatever they wished.

Television shows such as *Touched by an Angel* reflect the cultural notion that God does miracles for people regardless of what they believe and the way they live. And, we shall learn, the miracles at shrines perpetuate the same idea. This is so important that in a future chapter we will consider the topic in more detail.

Prayer and God's Will

God does miracles today in answer to prayer and in accordance with His own will.

> *Is any one of you in trouble? He should pray. Is anyone happy? Let him sing songs of praise. Is any one of you sick? He should call the elders of the church to pray over him and anoint him with oil in the name of the Lord. And the prayer offered in faith will make the sick person well; the Lord will raise him up. If he has sinned, he will be forgiven. Therefore confess your sins to each other and pray for each other so that you may be healed. (James 5:13–16)*

James cannot be interpreted to mean that a believer will always be raised up; logic would again require that we could thereby escape death. The answer to this prayer is dependent on "the prayer of faith," which means that in specific instances God may grant the elders united faith to believe in the restoration of an individual; in other instances, they might not have such faith. The "raising up" takes place only when God grants the gift of faith for that particular situation. It is impossible for us to manufacture such faith on our own.

Notice also the connection between the physical healing and the confession of sins. Here again we have a powerful argument against the idea that healing is available to all, no questions asked. It has been my experience that God sometimes raises people up in answer to prayer and sometimes He does not. At the end of the day, we must leave it in His hands. As Jesus Himself prayed, "May your will be done" (Matthew 26:42).

Miracles in the name of Jesus, for the glory of God, do take place today. But if we are to "prove all things," as Paul tells us (1 Thessalonians 5:21 KJV), we must be willing to investigate to see if the experience meets biblical criteria. Surely in our confused day, discernment is more important than ever. *We can be quite sure that miracles done in the name of Jesus are for those who have accepted Jesus as their Savior and Lord and walk in obedience to His will.*

God help us to have the divine balance: "Do not put out the Spirit's fire; do not treat prophecies with contempt. Test everything. Hold on to the good. Avoid every kind of evil" (1 Thessalonians 5:19–22).

NOTES

Portions of this chapter first appeared in *Seven Convincing Miracles: Understanding the Claims of Christ in Today's Culture,* by Erwin W. Lutzer (Chicago: Moody, 1999).

1. *Chicago Sun-Times,* 12 October 1998, 11.
2. Helen Schuchman, *A Course in Miracles* (Glen Ellyn, Ill.: Foundation for Inner Peace, 1992), viii.
3. B. B. Warfield, *Counterfeit Miracles* (London: Banner of Truth, 1918), 3.
4. Ibid.
5. Ibid., 20.
6. Ibid., 26.
7. Hudson Taylor, cited by K. Neil Foster, *Sorting Out the Supernatural* (Camp Hill, Pa.: Christian Publications, 2001), 8.
8. Peter Wagner, *How to Have a Healing Ministry Without Making Your Church Sick!* (Ventura, Calif.: Regal, 1989), 228; cited by John H. Armstrong, "In Search of Spiritual Power," in Michael Scott Horton, ed., *Power Religion: The Selling Out of the Evangelical Church?* (Chicago: Moody, 1992), 74.
9. Bob Jones, "Visions and Revelations"; audiotape, 1989; cited by John H. Armstrong, "In Search of Spiritual Power," *Power Religion,* 75.
10. John Wimber, cited by C. Peter Wagner, *The Third Wave of the Holy Spirit* (Ann Arbor, Mich.: Servant, 1999), 96; in John H. Armstrong, "In Search of Spiritual Power," *Power Religion,* 76.
11. John H. Armstrong, "In Search of Spiritual Power," *Power Religion,* 76.

12. John Wimber, Church Planting Seminar (3 audiotapes, 1981); cited by John Goodwin in *Media Spotlight* (1990), 24; in John H. Armstrong, "In Search of Spiritual Power," *Power Religion*, 76–77.

13. Alan Cole, *The Southern Cross* (April 1987), 13 (emphasis his); cited by D. A. Carson in "The Purpose of Signs and Wonders in the New Testament," *Power Religion*, 95.

14. Don Carson, "The Purpose of Signs and Wonders in the New Testament," *Power Religion*, 95.

15. Ibid., 94.

16. Charles Farah, "A Critical Analysis: The 'Roots and Fruits' of Faith-Formula Theology," in D. A. Carson, ed., *Showing the Spirit: A Theological Exposition of 1 Corinthians 12–14* (Grand Rapids: Baker, 1987), 177.

17. D. A. Carson, *Showing the Spirit*, 39–40.

6

WHEN YOU JUDGE ENTERTAINMENT

How Much of Hollywood Should We Let into Our Homes?

How would you react if someone were to break into your home and kidnap your children? You say, "Well, thankfully, that won't happen; our doors are locked, the alarm is on, and the police are available to catch the criminal." You would be willing to die to protect your children.

What if I were to tell you that children—yes, even children in Christian homes—are being stolen, right from within their homes? The Enemy comes through locked doors and bolted windows. To be sure, the bodies of the children are left in the home, but their hearts have been lured to serve other masters. Their allegiance is transferred to what the apostle Paul called "the god of this world" (2 Corinthians 4:4 NASB).

More surprising is that many parents are in cahoots with these thieves. They cooperate through their own support and participation in the Enemy's battle plan. If children in their early twenties were stolen, we might argue that they are old enough to fend for themselves; but young children, ages twelve and thirteen, are being lured away while their parents tend to the matter of living and are consumed with their own agendas.

In this chapter we enter into the realm ruled by the god of this world. The contents of this chapter will be accepted by many, but unfortunately, I wonder how many will change their lifestyles as a result of reading this material. Those who are already hooked by the entertainment industry have difficulty separating themselves from those things that corrode the soul. Truth be told, we are all in danger of selling out to the god of this world.

Who are these thieves that have come to capture the hearts of our children and already rule the hearts of many adults? In a word, they are the various media outlets, the entertainment industry that has targeted our children for a massive takeover. Yes, that includes movies, the Internet, and the music industry.

When we attend a movie, we think that we are just being entertained; but the fact is that we are being educated. Our values and attitudes are either being elevated or destroyed; either the education is for our good or, ultimately, for our harm. If Hollywood makes an R-rated movie, with sex and violence, producers know that teenagers will see it. Indeed, 80 percent of teens under seventeen say they have been able to see R-rated movies.[1] These movies, regardless of their rating and content, will shape their opinion of what constitutes normal sexual behavior; the movies will influence attitudes regarding integrity, violence, and values. So within the counterfeit world created by the producers, powerful feelings are unleashed.

While they are in the theater, teens are being educated in how to treat the opposite gender, how they should dress, the value of life, and what is important in the world. Movie ratings are meaningless. First, because the producers push the limit, always wanting to expand the boundaries of decency; and second, because even a G-rated movie can have themes of rebellion, occultism, and questionable morality. In fact, the rating system has actually contributed to our moral toboggan slide. All that a producer has to do is have his show get a PG-13 rating, and then he can pretty well produce whatever he pleases. Larry Poland of Mastermedia says of the rating board, "It's a case of the fox guarding the chicken."

"We want people to laugh at adultery, homosexuality and incest," said one scriptwriter, "because laughing breaks down your resistance to it." Think about this: Far more than half the children under eighteen have seen X-rated movies and 25 percent tried to copy what they saw within days of seeing the material.[2] No wonder you have twelve-year-old children trying to molest other children. One television program spent the whole hour making one point: If you are a teenager and not having sex, you probably are gay. Think of the destructive messages being sent to our children!

In addition to immorality and violence, many TV programs are now dedicated to promoting the occult. Shows feature witches, spells, and magic of various sorts. Since occultism is having so much influence through the media and our culture, an entire chapter will be devoted to it later in this book.

Next we have rap music with its dirty lyrics, obscene language, and violent sexual images. These words and feelings embed themselves into the minds of teenagers; words and images loaded with immoral values and impulses find a home within their hearts. Most of us who are older don't have any idea of the obscenities and ideas communicated through this powerful medium. Taken together, multiplied millions of rap albums are sold each year, many containing the most vulgar, base, degrading, exploitative, and violent images one can imagine.

> THE LEVEL OF HOS-
> TILITY AND ANGER
> AGAINST RELIGION
> IN THE ENTERTAIN-
> MENT INDUSTRY IS
> VERY EVIDENT.

Think of what it means to have these degrading influences seep into the homes of this nation. We are surprised when teenagers commit crimes, but should we be? In the eighteenth century, Andrew Fletcher, a Scottish patriot and anti-Unionist, famously said, "If a man were permitted to make all the ballads, he need not care who should make the laws of a nation."[3]

MTV, with its emphasis on sex—any kind of sex with whomever, whenever—is faithfully watched by millions of teenagers, who identify with the images and powerful sexual expressions. What a boy once felt sexually when he was seventeen, he now feels at the age of twelve. Many men who are slaves to pornography say that they were introduced to it at the age of twelve or thirteen, and once they embarked on the road of sexual fantasies, they found themselves simultaneously both liking it and hating it. Yet, try as they might, they could not free themselves from one or more kinds of sexual addiction.

The cautions and restraints of previous generations are gone. Young women are embarrassed to say that they are virgins. Young men exploit young women and ridicule those who hold to standards of decency. So deeply has sexual deviancy become a part of our society that parents cannot trust the teachers of their children, and children cannot trust other children. No wonder the Centers for Disease Control reports that there are forty thousand new cases of sexually transmitted disease each and every day in America.

The Internet, with all of its potential for good, has also opened the door to pornography and trash. Just this week a Christian mother told me that her son began to access child pornography and now is in jail for acting out on what he saw. One Christian man gave a testimony to twenty-eight men in a Bible study, telling of how God delivered him from Internet pornography. Twenty-two in the group admitted to sampling porn on the Internet and struggling with the same issues.

Of course, Hollywood and the producers of pornography say that all this is just entertainment and does not affect behavior. That's foolish, when you think of the billions of dollars spent on television ads every year. If commercials do not affect what we do, why is big money spent on them? Every sex crime imaginable has been influenced by pornography. Fact is, we all know we are affected by what we see, and things are going to get worse, not better.

We cannot lay the blame for all of this on the doorsteps of Hollywood and the producers of pornography. They thrive because there is a market for their products; they appeal to our baser instincts, knowing that human beings tend to gravitate toward the path of least resistance. They are simply taking advantage of our fallen nature and exploiting our penchant to fulfill our desires. They find it profitable to destroy decency at every level. I'm reminded of the words of G. K. Chesterton, who said that *meaninglessness does not come from being weary of pain, but meaninglessness comes from being weary of pleasure.*

If you are counting on them to take some responsibility, don't hold your breath. The entertainment industry does not care about values other than its own. It is driven by profits. And their aim is to ensnare your child so that he will be addicted to the music, sex, pornography, and violence of the media. If so, they can count on his being one of their clients for the rest of his life.

> WE ARE NOT HELPLESS IF WE ARE CREATIVE AND COURAGEOUS.

Movie critic Michael Medved says that the level of hostility and anger against religion in the entertainment industry is very evident. The producers disdain anyone who holds to biblical values or even to what could be loosely called "family values." If Christians are portrayed in the media, they are often shown to be hypocrites, unworthy of respect or serious consideration. Why don't we just accept the fact that, for the most part, those who produce entertainment are not our friends but greedy people who thrive on wealth and fame?

These, then, are the monsters that are coming into our homes and stealing the hearts of our children. Under the rubric of "entertainment," children, teenagers, and adults see, hear, and feel the impact of degrading values and images. Many good children, from both Christian and non-Christian homes, are at risk—they face the daily bombardment of the media that is intentionally leading them down destructive paths.

OUR PARALYSIS

If the situation is even partially as bad as I have made it out to be, why don't we do something about it? I'm not talking about marches on Hollywood or boycotts of theaters, though that might have some limited value. But the fact is that we have to do something for ourselves if we care about our children and grandchildren.

Why don't we act?

First, we are in denial. We know that the problem is out there, but because it seems to be so overwhelming we think that if we look the other way, it will go away. Parents are intimidated, fearing what will happen if they try to exercise some authority over their children. We hope that, if we pray, God will somehow protect our young people. In our hearts we hope that in some inexplicable way they won't be influenced by what they see. It is a fruitless wish.

At the end of this chapter, I will give specific suggestions on what can be done for our children—and for us. We are not helpless if we are creative and courageous. We simply cannot submit to the Enemy and yet entertain the hope that we will win the battle. Too much is at stake, and what is more, we are representatives of Almighty God. He has not left us powerless to stand against the onslaughts of the world.

Second, we as adults are guilty. We don't want to be too hard on our children, lest we have to clean up our own act. One man, who saw that his twelve-year-old son was fascinated with the pictures of the Swimsuit Issue of *Sports Illustrated*, found himself speechless, since he (the father) subscribed to the magazine and also spent time ogling the pictures. So we prefer to believe that there is nothing to be alarmed about. We have lost our moral authority because, in our hearts, we know that we are just as vulnerable to the lusts of this world as our children.

I think of the parent who said, "My kid is all messed up from heavy metal music and exposure to sexual videos on MTV at an early age. But you can't blame *me* for his problems. I'm never home."[4] So rather than stepping up to the plate as parents, we back away, finding excuses and hoping for the best. Christian parents think they can safely watch pornography and violence and justify it by saying, "I'm just watching it; I'd never *do* it."

> WHEN SIN HAS CONTROL, SELF-PROTECTION AND SELF-FULFILLMENT BECOME OUR PRIMARY OCCUPATIONS.

Third, we don't understand the battle. We simply do not realize that our real enemy is not Hollywood, nor the pornographers, nor those who do vulgar rap music. We might be able to stand against those forces and win; but when we enter the devil's territory we are in hand-to-hand combat. This is where he rules; this is where he exercises his power and claims dominion. In fact, I'm sure the devil even twists the biblical text that he is the "god of this world," insisting that Christians have no right to encroach on his territory. He will fight us to the death, *our* death. But overcome him we can—and must.

TESTING WHAT COMES INTO OUR HOMES

So: How much of Hollywood should we allow in our homes? Where do we draw the line? And how can we help our children plough a straight furrow in a crooked world? Let me introduce you to three tests that will help us decide what is appropriate and what is not. Whatever material passes these three tests can be confidently allowed into your home and mine.

The time has come for strong medicine. But the medicine, if that's what we call it, comes directly from the Scriptures. We really don't have the right to accommodate ourselves to the spirit of the age if we want this prayer answered for ourselves and our families: "May your whole spirit, soul and body be kept blameless at the coming of our Lord Jesus Christ. The one who calls you is faithful and he will do it" (1 Thessalonians 5:23–24).

It is very hypocritical for a person to laugh at something that makes God angry. It is hypocritical for us to see and participate in what grieves our Lord. Either we will accept God's standard or be drawn into the seductive power of the world.

The Content Test

Our first test is the *content* test, asking ourselves if the movie, video, or Internet material that comes into our home pleases the Lord.

Do not love the world or anything in the world. If anyone loves the world, the love of the Father is not in him. For everything in the world—the cravings of sinful man, the lust of his eyes and the boast-ing of what he has and does—comes not from the Father but from the world. The world and its desires pass away, but the man who does the will of God lives forever. (1 John 2:15–17)

James makes the same point, "You adulterous people, don't you know that friendship with the world is hatred to-ward God? Anyone who chooses to be a friend of the world becomes an enemy of God" (James 4:4). Just imagine: If we choose the world for our friend, we make God our enemy. Every day we are forced to take sides.

What is this world we are warned not to love?

First, John refers to the "cravings of sinful man," that is, the forbidden sexual desires that cover a wide range of ex-pressions: pornography, adultery, homosexuality, lust, and the like.

Second, there is the "lust of the eyes," which might also include sexual stimuli, but at the heart of this expression is covetousness, that is, desiring what is not ours. The advertising industry knows that it can count on us to want what others have, so they try to make us dissatisfied with everything from toothpaste to cars—so dissatisfied that we will opt for the brand being advertised.

> SATAN DOES NOT RESPOND TO SWEET REASON.

Then, there is pride, the "boasting of what he has or does," which can be defined as self-absorption. To love the world is, at root, to worship the goddess of self, that is, our tendency to satisfy legitimate desires in the wrong way. When sin has control, self-protection and self-fulfillment become our primary occupations.

What does God think of these three expressions of our fallen nature? Speaking of the person who follows these paths, John says, "The love of the Father is not in him." As quoted above, James puts it even more strongly, saying that to love the world is to become God's enemy.

We've all had the experience of watching a risqué television program, and if we are sensitive to the Holy Spirit, we can almost feel our love for God drain from our souls. We have that inner sense of impurity, the conviction that we have violated God's highest desire for us. Worse, we are aware that that the One we love has been grieved.

Why is the love of the world so serious? If we love sin, we not only love what God hates, we love what put Jesus on the cross. Let us suppose that your son was murdered; would you keep the knife that killed him in a special case so that it could be admired? Would you tell your friends, "Just look how sharp that blade is; and look at its beautiful symmetry!" Just so, when we love sin, we love what killed Jesus.

Realize that Satan is behind this assault on biblical values. The first instance of violence in the Bible was satanic. Cain killed Abel, and the New Testament identifies the murderer as being "of the evil one" (1 John 3:12 NASB). The immorality of the people preceding the Flood was a satanic onslaught. Indeed, it appears that the spirits that were actively inspiring all forms of immoral behavior were so wicked that they are now confined to Tartarus ("hell," 2 Peter 2:4 NASB). So today, we are involved in satanic conflict.

Satan does not respond to sweet reason; he does not play by the rules, so he will not go down without a fight. He wants to rule this world and have it drown in sensuality and rebellion. He is determined that we as Christians become unwilling partners with his agenda. Information itself won't change us. To ask people—even Christians—to give up the sins that feed their desires is asking for a battle. Perhaps the reason we think the biblical standard is so high is that we have fallen so low.

How much of Hollywood should you let into your home? Run it past the content test: Does it ignite my innate desires for the lust of the flesh, the lust of the eyes, or the pride of life? Is this the kind of music or movie I would watch if I had Jesus over for dinner?

At the end of this chapter I'll give some practical suggestions along with spiritual direction that might help in stemming the onslaught. The war for the minds of this generation is winnable. We just have to fight it on many fronts.

The Control Test

Richard Price said in *Movieline:* "There is only one thing more powerful than dope and that is movies."[5] Of course if a movie passes the content test, it will be the kind we can invite into our homes. But even then, it has the potential of controlling our lives and hindering our relationship with God.

Paul put forward the control test: "'Everything is permissible for me'—but not everything is beneficial. 'Everything is permissible for me'—but I will not be mastered by anything" (1 Corinthians 6:12). Apparently, Paul was responding to a slogan that was used to justify certain immoral practices; but he qualifies it to say that even if something is permissible, that does not make it right in and of itself. Whatever controls us, is sin. There is a form of liberty that is slavery.

As men, we have difficulty controlling the TV zapper. We love to channel surf, and more often than not, our eyes focus on sensual scenes. We love to tell ourselves that we are in control; we can turn to whatever channel we want to! Yes, just look at how we can control that zapper; we can go directly from *News Watch* to *Baywatch* with just one click of a button! And so we tell ourselves lies we want to believe.

> THE MORE TIME WE HAVE, THE MORE "THINGS" WE CRAM INTO THE EMPTY SPACES.

I know some men who are absorbed with sports; they are obsessed with football, basketball, or baseball, or all three. Though sports might pass the content test, the fact is that such absorption can interfere with one's relationship with God. Richard Keyes was right when he wrote, "An idol is something within creation that is inflated to function as a substitute for God. All sorts of things are potential idols. . . . An idol can be a physical object, a property, a person, an activity, a role, an institution, a hope, an image, an idea, a pleasure, a hero."[6]

If we simply define idolatry as something that gives us more fulfillment than God, we are all idolaters of one kind or another. And it is this idolatry that God hates; He wants nothing greater in our lives than He. Surely, when our lives are filled with entertainment, even good entertainment, we find less time to concentrate on those things that are most important. God is grieved when we do not find Him to be satisfying.

If you think you are in control of your television set, prove it by keeping it off for a week. You can keep up with the news by reading the daily newspaper and listening to the radio. The fact is that television is such a great part of our lives that many of us would find it difficult to stop watching, even for a brief time. We don't know whether we are addicted until we try to quit. No wonder a friend of mine finally decided to cut the electrical cord of his TV, knowing that this was the only hope of ending his fascination with the "one-eyed monster."

Let's answer this question candidly: Are we in control of the entertainment we allow into our lives? Or are we driven —perhaps even obsessed—with the need for movies, music, or the Internet? Even the good can be the enemy of the best.

The Clock Test

What is the clock test? "Be very careful, then, how you live—not as unwise but as wise, making the most of every opportunity, because the days are evil" (Ephesians 5:15). Suppose a movie passes the content test, and even the control test, we still might not be free to enjoy it.

When Paul says that we should "make the most of every opportunity," the Greek phrase is that we must *redeem* the time; that is, we must buy the time out of the marketplace. There are so many demands for our time today that we have to make time for the things that matter to God.

Many years ago when my wife and I were in Eastern Europe, the people had to stand in line to buy food—perhaps an hour to buy meat, then another hour for a loaf of bread, and the like. In all, we were told that the average family had someone stand in line for about three hours a day just to purchase the basics. Some of the Christians told us how fortunate we were because those of us who lived in America had so much more time to pray and serve God!

But it doesn't work that way, does it? My experience has been that technology has not given us more time to serve God, for the more time we have, the more "things" we cram into the empty spaces. Unfortunately, developing our relationship with God and His people is often marginalized, no matter how much time our high-tech society gives us.

Let's ask ourselves some hard questions: Are we satisfied with the way we spent our time last year? Let's evaluate the return of our investment for the number of hours we sat in front of the television set during the last twelve months. Did the time spent make us a better person? Did it improve our character? Imagine what we would be like if we had spent all that time, say, reading our Bible and becoming involved in the needs in our community!

Most heartbreaking is how retirees spend their last years. I've known many who sit in front of the television set, day after day, year after year. One man, weary with television, decided that he would like to do something for Jesus before he died. So he got a missionary list from his church and wrote personal letters to seventy missionaries. He kept in touch with each one, prayed for them, and spent his final years profitably.

Let's remember that the Lord will not say, "Well done, thou good and faithful servant, for thou hast watched 5,312 hours of television!" We only get one shot at life; when a single hour is gone, it can never be retrieved. So we must ask: How do I want to spend the few short years and hours on this planet, knowing that I will have to give an account to our Lord?

With these questions in mind, we are in a better position to decide how much of Hollywood should be allowed into our home.

MAKING HARD DECISIONS

Knowing that we are up against a power that is greater than ourselves, we must prayerfully take some steps to limit, if not eliminate, the impact of the entertainment industry in our own lives and the lives of our children. We have to respect our homes, the place where attitudes are formed and lifestyles developed.

Here are some general comments before I give more specifics.

1. *We must clean up our own act before we can help others.* Each of us must make a decision of conscience: From what aspect of the world does the Lord want to free me? As I've mentioned at the beginning of this book, we cannot keep others from drowning if we ourselves are going under. Our greatest need is to live a righteous life personally, to make sure that our own house is clean and empty. Only then can it be filled with the goodness God has implanted within the lives of those who believe.

I've often wondered why Christians who complain so much about the content of television spend so much time watching it. So, let's ask: What steps are we willing to take to confront this monster? Are we willing to cancel our subscription to cable television? Are we willing to make strict limits for ourselves and have accountability to others? Can we do without television for a week? Two weeks?

Those of us who do not have children living at home must be strong for families that do. We have to reach out beyond ourselves, helping others through dialogue, personal caring, and prayer. Together we have to accept the challenge of being pure in this impure culture.

2. *We must set a family standard.* "Parents who provide their children with a clear standard of right and wrong empower them to make the best personal and moral choices throughout their life."[7] These standards must be objective, not based on personal preference. Children will argue that just because you don't like Madonna videos or slasher films that doesn't make them wrong for those who "appreciate" them. We must help children see that our standards are based on biblical absolutes, not just personal taste.

Ken Myers says that the present cultural onslaught is potentially more insidious to the Christian's welfare than outright persecution. He says, "Enemies that come loudly and visibly are usually much easier to fight than those that are undetectable. . . . The erosion of character, the spoiling of innocent pleasures and the cheapening of life itself that often accompany modern popular culture can occur so subtly that we believe nothing has happened."[8] Our insensitivity to God's standard is proof of how far we have drifted.

3. *We must talk with our children about what they are seeing and hearing.* If you have a TV in your home, or even if you don't, you can be quite sure that your children are being exposed to the "thieves" we have described. We have to listen to the songs, listen to the lyrics, and see the movies. Young people rebel when we simply announce that from today on,

things are going to be different. If you do not understand
where they are coming from, educate yourself.

Do I as a parent have to expose myself to this impurity?
Do I have to listen to the perverted sexual references, the dialogue, and the music? The answer is yes; after all, if you
can't handle it, what makes you think your child can?

Please don't think that I am contradicting the "tests" I've
described in this chapter. Of course, it would be best if we
would never have to listen to rap music or see degrading
films, but if your child is into it, as a parent you had better
become acquainted with what your child is hearing and seeing. As Josh McDowell says, "Rules without relationship
leads to rebellion."

Communication with teenagers about all kinds of subjects is absolutely necessary if we hope to guide them
through this world to a genuine love for God. We should
talk to them about television and about their interests. We
must enter their world to gain credibility; we must get to
know their turf. We must learn to enjoy them and have fun
together.

We must affirm our children as individuals.[9] Only when
we have listened to them and gained their trust can we answer some of their objections to our beliefs. Be prepared for
statements such as: "OK, so the words are immoral, but the
musician probably didn't mean it!" Or, "You have to understand that this is just a movie and not reality." Or again,
"You know that what people accept is constantly changing,
so the problem is that you just belong to a different generation." We must help the children "find the lie" in what they
watch and hear.[10]

Negative warnings alone do not work. You can warn

them, threaten them, and condemn them, and they will continue to follow their desires. And the more you condemn them, the more they will be driven into their own secret world of sensuality. You must prove in your own life that a walk with Christ is satisfying. Reason might change someone's mind, but it will never change the heart.

Your convictions must be accompanied with nonjudgmental communication, where the child feels he can discuss his deepest longings, temptations, and fears. If he knows in advance that he will be condemned, his heart will be closed rather than open to what you have to say.

> DON'T CLOSE YOUR BIBLE UNTIL YOU HAVE SOMETHING FROM IT THAT WILL FILL YOUR SOUL FOR THAT DAY.

Also, combine your concerns with examples from your own life of how you have fallen into temptation and the lessons (often bitter) that you learned as a result. I have marveled at how we as parents often expect our children to live up to standards that we ourselves have not kept. Some parents continue to fail in the very matter where they expect their children to succeed. The more realistic we are about our own struggles and sins, the more likely our children will believe that we are real; they will respect us rather than write us off as people who simply do not understand.

Of course children will exploit inconsistencies. The parent who forbids his child to attend an R-rated movie but sits at home watching trash or rents R-rated videos—such parents undermine their moral authority. So often, when children stray from the faith and take a nosedive into the world, I wonder what lesson God wants to teach the parents. Perhaps it is because of their own inconsistencies; or perhaps it is because the parents thought that nagging, cajoling, and warnings could actually change the child. Let us always remember that we cannot change others; we can direct children in the right path, but when they come of age, they must make their parents' convictions their own.

4. *Take practical steps.* According to Robert DeMoss, 60 percent of all teenagers have a TV in their bedroom, where they can watch all the television they like, unsupervised, without restraint, and without accountability.[11] He recommends, and I agree, that no child should have a TV in his or her bedroom. It is important that the television set be in a public room in the house, where it can be monitored. Then your child can't be watching TV without your knowing what he is watching and doing.

5. *Those who have young children should establish rules early.* Block out MTV. Buy wholesome videos and give your child a healthy diet of what is good and right. Prepare your children for the fact that you will never be able to protect them completely from influences such as rap music and pornography.

For example, while rummaging through a garbage dump, two boys came across a stash of pornography. They began regular visits to the site, until they began behaving strangely. Their parents picked up on this, and when they questioned the boys, the truth came out. The wrong thing to do would have been to shame them or to make them feel as though they had committed the unpardonable sin. We must remember that shame only focuses the mind and heart on the sin itself.

The boys already felt shamed and guilty. Their wise mother helped them process their guilt; she helped them understand the natural attraction they would have toward such material, along with its dangers; but most important, she helped them understand the forgiveness and cleansing of Christ. She knew, as any mother in today's world should, that this would probably not be the last time they would see such material, either by accident or choice.

Explain to your children how they will be tempted; they will be exposed to material that will arouse both their curiosity and their sexual desires. Help them understand, as well, that though their desires are God-given, trying to satisfy those desires through pornography will lead to a distortion of God's best for them.

Since everyone wants to be "empowered" these days, empower your children to leave a friend's home where inappropriate movies are being shown, or where there is drinking and the like. Our children need our support and empowerment to turn away from the temptations of the world.

6. *Practice the spiritual disciplines.* Pray, pray, pray! Learn the Word of God; it will guard your heart and mind in Christ Jesus. Don't close your Bible until you have something from it that will fill your soul for that day. I've had the good fortune of having parents who have prayed for me regularly. In addition, as a pastor I've had prayer partners who pray for me, knowing that I need their support and prayers. Within the church we must enlist others to pray for us and be accountability partners.

In A.D. 1635 an Arab chief nicknamed "Farras the horseman" was traveling through the desert with a large herd of horses. Suddenly, in the distance a body of water came into view. The herd, crazed by thirst, broke into a stampede, racing toward the stream. Farras tested the obedience of the animals by blowing loudly on his horn, sounding the call to battle. Out of that great herd, five horses stopped in their tracks, wheeled around, and returned to obey the call. These five mares, the story goes, became the stock of the world-famous Arabian horses.

Our nation is dashing madly toward a distant mirage. Even we in the church have been caught up in the quest for entertainment that saps our time and dampens our love for God. The Almighty has sounded the alarm; He looks for a few to return and stand for Him at great personal cost, despite the temptations and challenges of our culture.

Will we be among those who will answer His call?

NOTES

1. Robert G. DeMoss Jr., *Learn to Discern* (Grand Rapids: Zondervan, 1992), 9. (Many ideas in this chapter on how to control the media in our homes come from this very helpful book).
2. *Death by Entertainment: How the Media Manipulates the Masses* (Hemet, Calif.: Jeremiah Films, 2000), videotape.
3. Andrew Fletcher of Saltoun, "An Account of a Conversation Concerning a Right Regulation of Government for the Good of Mankind. In a Letter to the Marquis of Montrose" (1704); in *Political Works* (1732), pt. 7.
4. DeMoss, *Learn to Discern*, 12.
5. *Death by Entertainment.*
6. Richard Keyes, quoted in Ronald Dunn, *Surviving Friendly Fire* (Nashville: Thomas Nelson, 2001), 76.
7. DeMoss, *Learn to Discern*, 86.
8. Ibid., 89.
9. Ibid., 100.
10. Ibid., 103.
11. Ibid., 108.

WHEN YOU JUDGE APPEARANCES

What Is the Relationship Between Beauty and Happiness?

How attractive do you have to be before you have the right to "feel good about yourself"? And what can you expect if you were born with a rather ordinary appearance or with a physical disability? Is there a connection between beauty and happiness?

Our culture answers these questions decisively: you had better look attractive if you will be thought worthy of acceptance and expect to be happily married. If you are unfortunate enough to have arrived on planet Earth without the gift of beauty, you'd better do something about it or be thrown on the scrap heap of humanity. It's not who you *are* but how you *look* that matters.

"No one noticed my good grades and all of my achievements, until I had implants," said one woman. "Now I'm noticed by men. I knew I could never be happy unless I was beautiful."

"To me plastic surgery was like being converted to a new religion, and it demanded the same commitment and sacrifice," observes a thirty-something woman. "But it was worth it," she says, now that she can see her customized body, shaped by innumerable surgeries. "It's my body, so I can do with it whatever I want . . . if I want to look a certain way, I have that right."

Now, comes word of a new injectable drug for cosmetic purposes that is predicted to work magic on the faces of America. This new drug promises that we will look at wrinkles the way we look at cracked or discolored teeth—as a remnant of the past. Indeed, the drug is so popular among actors that it is playing havoc with facial expressions—some say it is impossible to find an actor who can actually look angry! A drug for those who refuse to age.

We are besieged with dieting programs, used not so much for health reasons but to have a beautiful body so that we can "feel good about ourselves." Despite the obvious benefits of the exercise craze, the fact is that for many people it is the path to a slimmer, trimmer, and more sexy body. Of course I agree that we should eat right, exercise, and try to better our appearance. What I am steadfastly opposing is our culture's overemphasis on physical beauty to the neglect of the weightier matters of the spirit.

There is something profoundly wrong with our values when young women are starving themselves to death, trying to be thin. Looking "just right" becomes such an obsession that many become detached from reality, unable to process information with a minimum of objectivity. So focused are they on the shape of their bodies, that they see themselves differently than others do. I know a woman who was thin—on the verge of starvation—but when she looked into the mirror she saw herself as hopelessly overweight. In our image-obsessed world, many young people are quite literally "dying to be thin." We have a cult of "thin."

Enter the word *anorexia.*

This, someone has said, refers to starvation in a land of plenty. Seven million American girls and 1 million American boys struggle with eating disorders. Young women especially become obsessed with their weight and are trapped in the self-loathing despair of anorexia. Once entrenched, it is one of the most difficult eating disorders to treat. Of all psychiatric illnesses, it has the highest fatality rate. Peter Rowan writes:

> Anorexia is a problem in Western civilization, a problem for the prosperous. It is a question of being thirsty in the rain. Anorexia is both the result of and a protest against the cultural rule that young women must be beautiful. In the beginning, a young woman strives to be thin and beautiful, but after a time, anorexia takes on a life of its own. By her behavior an anorexic girl tells the world, "Look, see how thin I am, even thinner than you wanted me to be. You can't make me eat more. I am in control of my fate, even if my fate is starving."[1]

Because women know that men can see better than they can think, they carry an unbearable burden in a culture that is capable only of superficial judgments. "The premium for women on physical beauty over intelligence is on the order of 100 to 1," says psychologist Dr. Rex Beaber.[2]

Who is to blame for this obsession with physical appearance? Certainly part of the problem is that television

> TO ASSESS A PERSON'S CHARACTER IS MUCH MORE DIFFICULT THAN ASSESSING APPEARANCE.

and movies have magnified this false standard. The soaps feature the beautiful people of the world, the 1 or 2 percent who were born with a wonderful confluence of genes. The rest of us—the 90-something percent—do not rate such roles.

Recently there have been a number of "real life" programs where young men and women meet for the first time, trying in a few hours to assess whether they might have the basis for a future romance. Once again, only beautiful people are allowed to participate, perpetuating the myth that first impressions are essentially reliable and that attractiveness is the basis for choice. Such artificial standards of romance are destroying adolescents.

Bob DeMoss points out that it is to the advantage of the advertiser if every time you look into the mirror, you get the nagging message *You don't measure up!* Of course the answer is to have a makeover of some kind. The cosmetic industry has thought of some new way to make you look beautiful. Woe to those who do not take advantage of these "opportunities." These ads reduce women to what Madonna called "a boy toy."[3]

In an age obsessed with sex, we should not be surprised that our culture is besotted with the human body, the cult of beauty. If you don't look good in a bathing suit, you don't rate, and so you might just as well accept second-class status. If an adolescent girl falls short of looking like Jennifer Lopez, or if a boy does not resemble the likes of Brad Pitt,

then such young people are fatally flawed, destined to a life
of rejection and embarrassment. No wonder this nation has
what James Dobson calls "an epidemic of inferiority."

Chuck Swindoll writes about the feelings an adolescent
girl wrestles with when she compares herself to this false
standard:

> Each tiny zit assures her that leprosy is just around the cor-
> ner. And clothes? We're talking daily nervous breakdown.
> And she's got this body that won't make up its mind . . .
> plus the kids at school and the commercials on the tube
> and the magazines in the rack all team up in some kind of
> secret conspiracy that convinces your once easygoing little
> lass that she is horribly overweight, ugly beyond belief,
> and hopelessly condemned to a life of embarrassment.[4]

But let's not think that adolescents are the only ones
feeling the pressure to reach some unattainable goal of
beauty. Adults are caught up in the whirlwind of appearances, too. Cosmetic surgery is a multibillion dollar industry, as people of all shapes and sizes get their nips and tucks,
with the hope that they will stave off the rejection that
comes to those who simply do not rate. As Dobson says,
"We reserve our praise and admiration for a select few who
have been blessed at birth with the characteristics we value
most highly."[5] We all respond differently to a cute, attractive
child than we do to an ordinary, somewhat unattractive one.
At an early age, children already know when they are devalued. The attractive child sees the world as loving and accepting while the ugly duckling sees the world as cruel and
rejecting.

Why this obsession with appearances? We are born with a God-given desire for significance, and because we desperately want the approval of others, we will try to meet their standards of acceptance. And in a culture where beauty is prized above achievement and character, we will do whatever we must to try to meet the criteria. In our day, beauty, as Dobson says, is "the gold coin of human worth." If I enjoy looking at you, your value goes up; if you are not much to look at, your stock goes down.

To assess a person's character is much more difficult than assessing appearance. We are impatient with the process of getting to know people, their dreams, their values and ideas. So, if you don't have a cute face and symmetry; if your curves have become angles and your nose is too large for the rest of your face, you aren't what people are looking for. Like it or not, we are judged by this worldly standard.

How superficial!

This cult of beauty is unfair to the attractive child, who is given undo attention quite apart from his character. Attractive young women are sought out and misused by young men bent on satisfying their sexual cravings. It's not too strong to say that beauty can be a curse, a ticket to a life committed to superficial values and sensuality.

But this standard is also unfair to the large majority of us who simply do not measure up to the worldly standards of beauty. Dobson writes, "How unfair . . . to reward a child for something he has not earned, or worse, to destroy him for circumstances beyond his control."[6] As any child knows, the average person does not win Miss America contests; the less-than-beautiful are not chosen to be cheerleaders; those with a so-so appearance have fewer friends and might never get married.

No attack is as powerful as the attack against our personhood. Self-image lies at the heart of who we are. So if you can be convinced that you are a shameful specimen of humanity; if you think that you are so awful looking that you are fundamentally unloved and unlovable, then you will retreat within the shell of your negativity and never be free to do anything significant for God. The "unblessed" child can give no explanation, no defense. He looks the way he looks, and that is that.

> WE CANNOT MAKE PROGRESS IN OUR WALK WITH GOD UNLESS WE COME TO TERMS WITH OUR APPEARANCE.

As Christians we must live by a different standard. We must declare war against the superficial values of our culture and march to the beat of a different drummer. Both in rearing our children and interacting with the people we meet, we must judge others by a better standard. This chapter seeks to answer important questions that will help us discern a balance between proper care for the body and a proper emphasis on character. We will attempt to answer questions such as:

What role should physical characteristics play in defining who we are?

Is plastic surgery always wrong?

What about body piercing, whether for rings or tattoos?

How can we use our bodies for the glory of God?

What can we do to stand against the superficial values of our culture?

As Christians we oppose Plato's notion that the flesh is inherently evil and the body but a prison for the soul. Thanks to the Fall, sin has contaminated us, body, soul and spirit, but in our final redemption, we will be entirely restored—body included. Indeed, Paul prayed, "May God himself, the God of peace, sanctify you through and through. May your whole spirit, soul and body be kept blameless at the coming of our Lord Jesus Christ" (1 Thessalonians 5:23).

Although the soul and body separate at death, this separation cannot be permanent. At death, we respect the human body, tenderly placing it in the ground with the assurance that, as a seed, it will someday come forth to newness of life. At that time of resurrection, our bodies will be joined to soul and spirit, that we might be whole and complete. Far from denigrating the human body, the Bible gives it a place of honor. Indeed at the Incarnation, the Son assumed a human body, which He now has in heaven and will have forever.

A SCRIPTURAL VIEW OF THE BODY

The biblical account is both simple and profound. "The LORD God formed the man from the dust of the ground and breathed into his nostrils the breath of life, and the man became a living being" (Genesis 2:7). Man was created from the earth so that he could relate to this earthly existence; but he was also created with a spirit with which he could communicate with God. This act of creation is the starting point for a scriptural view of the body.

God Created the Human Body

Self-acceptance, that is, accepting ourselves as God created us, lies at the heart of our sense of well-being and spiritual development. But even the beautiful people we've talked about have misgivings and self-doubt when they look into the mirror. We've all wondered where God was when we were put together. We cannot make progress in our walk with God unless we come to terms with our appearance; that is, unless we accept our appearance with gratitude.

The foundation of such self-acceptance is the sure knowledge that we were created by God, formed according to His specifications in our mother's wombs.

> *For you created my inmost being;*
> *you knit me together in my mother's womb.*
> *I praise you because I am fearfully and wonderfully made;*
> *your works are wonderful,*
> *I know that full well.*
> *My frame was not hidden from you*
> *when I was made in the secret place.*
> *When I was woven together in the depths of the earth,*
> *your eyes saw my unformed body.*
> *All the days ordained for me*
> *were written in your book*
> *before one of them came to be.*
>
> (Psalm 139:13–16)

There is no doubt that God regards a fetus as a baby, for He spoke of the prophet Isaiah before he was born: "Before I was born the LORD called me; from my birth he has made mention of my name" (Isaiah 49:1). Yes, the prophet affirmed that God formed him in the womb (44:24). The implications of God's direct involvement in our creation are important for us to understand.

This doctrine of creation means that we are born with what Bill Gothard calls the "unchangeables," that is, those features over which we have no control.[7] Certain basics were chosen for me by God, and I must accept them as part of His wise and loving provisions. If He had wanted any one of us to look like Cindy Crawford or Robert Redford, He could have chosen to create us thus; it appears as if He has not chosen to do so, and in that we must rest content.

What are some of those "unchangeables"?

First, the features of your body are God-given. Of course, as we know, children have an uncanny resemblance to their parents, but then we must remember that God created our parents too. Through them, God determined your height, the color of your eyes, your feet, hearing, hair, and the like. Now, of course, we might want to improve or change some of those features as best we can (change in hair color is probably the easiest to accomplish), but the raw material is a given. We must say, "Thank You, Father. I accept my features as from Your wise and loving hand."

Is not our modern obsession with trying to improve our features a latent rebellion against God? An ad in a newspaper read, "Introducing the eyes you wish you had been born with!" But is it too much to suggest that if God had wanted us to be born with different-colored eyes, He would have given them to us? My point is not to say that cosmetic surgery is always wrong or that working toward a slim body is sinful; rather, I affirm that the vain motivation that often accompanies such "improvements" is at odds with the will and purpose of the Creator.

Second, our racial mix, which includes the color of our skin, was determined by God. The history of the world includes war between the races; one race believes it deserves to be served by another. This conflict results in feelings of either inferiority or superiority. The Scriptures would affirm that no one should reject his racial background, for race is God's gift to the human family. Blessed

> WHAT OTHERS DESPISE, GOD IS PLEASED TO HONOR.

are those who are content with who they were born to be, neither wanting to lord it over others nor feeling that one is condemned because of his racial mix.

Third, God determined our limitations, defects, and deformities. When Moses was complaining about returning to Egypt because he did not have the gift of speech (possibly an impediment), God declared, "Who gave man his mouth? Who makes him deaf or mute? Who gives him sight or makes him blind? Is it not I, the LORD?" (Exodus 4:11).

You may ask: Why did God create me with a disability? Or, Why did He create me with limited mental capacities? We must also accept this as part of His divine will and wise purpose. Obviously, this does not mean that we cannot help those who were created with deformities, for we know that sin has marred God's creation. The fact that Jesus healed many is proof that we should do whatever is necessary to improve our physical condition. But those who strive against God because of their limitations hurt only themselves, rejecting the sovereign plan of God.

Finally, God chose our gender. Yes, He determined whether you and I would be a man or a woman. There is no doubt in my mind that sex-change operations are an attack against the image of God formed in every human being. It is He who created us, "male and female"; thus, to change from one gender to another is a form of rebellion against the Creator. In Old Testament times, cross-dressing was forbidden (Deuteronomy 22:5).

We dare not believe that the Almighty made a mistake when men were created as men, and women as women. In some cultures, women are despised and enslaved. Naturally, a woman in such circumstances might wish that she were born a man. Yet, blessed is she who can accept her sexuality, though she cannot condone the unfairness of her culture (nor can we).

> WE BELONGED TO GOD BY REASON OF *CREATION;* WE ALSO NOW BELONG TO GOD BY REASON OF *REDEMPTION.*

Accepting God's role in Creation helps us to accept one another without prejudice and without embarrassment. If I reject you because of your racial background, I am rebelling against the God who created you and chose that particular background for you. I'm saying, "God didn't know what He was doing when He created you black and me white." Racism is at root based in a notion of superiority that is offensive to God; and what is more, it is, in fact, rebellion against God. We should do all we can to include those who do not measure up to the artificial standards of beauty that the world so enthusiastically champions. We should not be put off by people just because they are unlike us; rather, we must intentionally reach out to people of all races, classes, and backgrounds. Every person is created in the image of God; every person is valuable to God and to us.

Parents, I must ask you: Are you embarrassed because your child does not meet some artificial criterion for human value? If your child does not look beautiful enough, is not smart enough, or has some disability—does that cause you to doubt your self-worth? Only those who are secure with how God made them are qualified to accept others as God made them. As Dobson says, it is not enough that you love your child; you must also respect him.[8]

In his book *What Kids Need Most in a Dad,* Tim Hansel tells a story about a teenager who had an obvious birthmark over much of his face. His self-esteem seemed secure; he related well with other students and was well liked. He had no self-consciousness about his appearance. Someone asked him how this could be?

He smiled and said, "When I was very young, my father started telling me that the birthmark was there for two reasons. One, it was where an angel kissed me; and two, the angel had done that so my father could always find me easily in a crowd." He continued, "My dad told me this so many times with so much love that as I grew up, I actually began to feel sorry for other kids who were not kissed by an angel like I was."[9]

In a book on discernment, I should point out that the father's theology was not literally correct; his son was not kissed by an angel. But his theology was completely correct in this regard: Birthmarks or what we call disabilities are not a judgment from God; they are not a curse, but they can be turned into a blessing if we accept them as from the hands of our loving heavenly Father. What others despise, God is pleased to honor; those who are not gifted with beauty can nevertheless be gifted with an abundance of divine favor and grace.

God wants us to understand that we should not strive with Him over how He created us. He wants us to be able to look into the mirror and see ourselves as creatures from His wise and loving hand. "Woe to him who quarrels with his Maker, to him who is but a potsherd among the potsherds on the ground. Does the clay say to the potter, 'What are you making?'" (Isaiah 45:9).

God Redeemed the Body

"Do you not know that your body is a temple of the Holy Spirit, who is in you, whom you have received from God? You are not your own; you were bought at a price. Therefore honor God with your body" (1 Corinthians 6:19–20). When we fell into sin, God chose to redeem us, knowing full well our condition and the cost we would be to Him. We were, said Paul, "bought with a price." Did Jesus die for us body, soul, and spirit? The answer is yes; He purchased us in our entirety. But our full inheritance awaits the day of resurrection.

We belonged to God by reason of *creation;* we also now belong to God by reason of *redemption.* In effect, we are "twice God's," for we can claim nothing of our own. The implications are clear: We do not have the right to say, "This is my body, I can do what I want with it." I have no more a right to do what I want with my own body than I have the right to do what I want with the money loaned to me by a friend who is expecting a return on his investment. The money is not mine to do with as I please; nor is my body mine to do with as I please.

Ever since we were born, we have begun the journey toward death, and this must be accepted as part of God's ordained plan. Signs of aging are a reminder that our days are numbered and we should apply our hearts unto wisdom. "Gray hair is a crown of splendor; it is attained by a righteous life" (Proverbs 16:31). Today's obsession with perpetual youth and beauty is modern man's attempt to deny the aging process. Some take this denial to an extreme, as one woman demonstrates. "I've spent a million dollars, and I've told my husband he should make sure I get a face-lift in the casket. I want to look good till I'm put away and never seen again."

Cosmetic surgery is not inherently sinful: we can applaud doctors who have taken deformed children and improved their features; we can understand changes made to approve one's appearance, but we cannot condone those who have makeovers of whatever sort in order to be more sexually provocative. Nor can we as Christians approve of changes made for the sake of vanity or on the assumption "This is my body; I can do with it as I please." The creature dare not usurp the ownership of the Creator.

What about body piercing, tattoos, and the like? Although tattoos were at one time symbols of rebellion found on the bodies of prison inmates and motorcycle gangs, these skin markings have now gone mainstream. The present mantra is that the human body is a canvas on which can be painted anything one pleases. We live in a sadistic, rebellious culture that wants to show that it can despoil the body. The early church was right when it saw tattoos as a desecration of the body. In the Old Testament we read, "'Do not cut your bodies for the dead or put tattoo marks on yourselves. I am the LORD'" (Leviticus 19:28).

Can a body covered with tattoos glorify God? Some young people, who thought the answer to that question might be yes, are changing their minds. One young woman I met said, "I'd give anything to have these tattoos removed, but they are permanent, and I had them done before I was saved. Now when I look at them, they are a reminder of my past life, which has been forgiven. I see them as my 'marks of grace.'" Yes, they can become marks of grace.

Women have worn earrings from earliest times. But today, we not only have earrings for men, but nose rings, lip rings, and navel rings. Never mind that tongue rings have been known to put poisons into the bloodstream and create grooves on teeth. Recently on the radio I heard a report about a Nebraska boy who holds the record for body piercing; the total, I think, was 135.

It is not my intention to make a definitive yes or no statement about these modern trends. It is, however, my express intention to say that today's emphasis on appearance and the lengths to which people are willing to go to be noticed are signs that our culture's values have drifted far from the security that comes from knowing God and submitting to His ownership.

We Are to Glorify God in Our Body

God created our bodies as a vehicle for His attributes: love, joy, and peace, to name a few. He wants to use our bodies as the means to a greater end, namely, the formation of Christian character and the spread of the gospel to the ends of the earth. We are His hands, His feet, His eyes, His ears. A body that is the temple of the Holy Spirit is a body that is used as a vessel, a holy place in which God dwells.

This is why Paul taught that the body itself did not have to look good in order for the treasure within it to shine forth. "But we have this treasure in jars of clay to show that this all-surpassing power is from God and not from us" (2 Corinthians 4:7).

> THINK OF WHAT WOULD HAPPEN IF EVERY ONE OF US CHOSE ONE OR TWO PEOPLE WE COULD BLESS AND AFFIRM.

Our bodies should be covered with modest clothing, so that we can be a compelling witness for Christ (see 1 Timothy 2:9–10). We should not strive to be the center of attention or draw our significance from special markings or expensive clothes. Our bodies were formed in the womb to be God's servants (Isaiah 49:5). And serving God is a full-time occupation.

Can a bodybuilder use his body for the "glory of God"? Depends. One such young man said, "I had to give up bodybuilding because I knew the reason I did it was to attract attention to myself, not to glorify God." The more intimate our relationship with God, the more likely we will be rebuked for our vanities.

CONCLUDING CHALLENGE

We've learned that we must learn to accept our bodies as from the hand of our wise and loving Creator. We must stand against a culture that glorifies the body and judges human beings by the standard of beauty and sexual attractiveness. What can we do to counteract these powerful trends and influences?

First, parents must consciously emphasize character, not appearance. When Samuel was sent to find a king among the sons of Jesse, the seven older brothers walked past the aging prophet, strutting their stuff. Yet, the Holy Spirit did not indicate that any one of them was to be the future king. Samuel was puzzled and inquired of the Lord, and then received a reply that should be emblazoned on the mind of every Christian, young or old. "Do not consider his appearance or his height, for I have rejected him. The Lord does not look at the things man looks at. *Man looks at the outward appearance, but the Lord looks at the heart*" (1 Samuel 16:7, emphasis added).

We parents must reward behavior, character, and faithfulness. We must intentionally communicate to this generation that there are some things more important than physical appearance. We must reach out to those young people who are terrified that they will be passed over in the "mating game." We must ourselves demonstrate that it is possible to have a relationship with God that is so satisfying that we do not have to compete in the unfair world of physical beauty. "Charm is deceptive, and beauty is fleeting; but a woman who fears the LORD is to be praised" (Proverbs 31:30).

Women should not base their self-worth on the number of men who notice them or, for that matter, on whether *anyone* notices them. Men should not base their self-worth on their popularity with women. Ultimately, we must draw our significance from who we are before God. We must steadfastly refuse to be drawn into the world's values at the very sensitive point of our physical appearance. We must be willing to please God, even if it means we disappoint those who mean the most to us.

Our churches have to help mothers who are trying to find modest clothes for their children. Our youth leaders and teachers must not favor those who are attractive but treat all as equals before God. Every one of us can make a difference by intentionally accepting and encouraging those who are least gifted in appearance. Think of what would happen if every one of us chose one or two people we could bless and affirm.

God prepared a body for Jesus, but what did He look like on earth? For centuries artists have tried to paint Him as they thought He must have looked, but they have nothing to go on except a knowledge of Middle Eastern culture and their own imaginations. Yet, the fact is we might have a clue to the appearance of Jesus given a description by the prophet Isaiah. What we learn is that Jesus might have been very ordinary in His appearance.

Just read this: "He had no beauty or majesty to attract us to him, nothing in his appearance that we should desire him" (Isaiah 53:2). If we take this description literally, Jesus was not a man with an attractive physique; He was not a handsome specimen of manhood. He was strikingly ordinary, and perhaps, if I might be forgiven for suggesting it, unattractive. And of course, when lacerated before the crucifixion, His body was so badly disfigured it was "marred beyond human likeness" (52:14).

He knew that His faithfulness to the Father's will was much more important than the appearance of His body; He knew that though He might not rate on the arbitrary scale of worldly values, He would yield Himself to the Father's will, and that was all that mattered.

This body—His ordinary body—would be used to touch a leper, to hold a child, and to speak the words of God. We see Him looking "beyond" the outward to the inward; He knew that a huge gap often exists between outward appearances and inward affections. This would be the body with which He would glorify the Father and purchase the salvation of all who would believe. This would be the body that would endure the sword in His side and the nail prints in His hands.

Jesus stands as a powerful rebuke to the body worship of our generation. He invites all who would follow Him to adopt a higher set of values; to look beyond the physical to the eternal, and to learn to accept others for who they are, and not how they look. "But we have this treasure in jars of clay to show that this all-surpassing power is from God and not from us" (2 Corinthians 4:7).

We must lead the way.

NOTES

1. Peter Rowan, cited in Mary Pipher, *Reviving Ophelia: Saving the Selves of Adolescent Girls* (New York: Ballantine, 1999), 174.
2. *People,* 30 October 2000, 108.
3. Robert G. DeMoss, *Learn to Discern* (Grand Rapids: Zondervan, 1992), 37.
4. Chuck Swindoll, *The Strong Family* (Portland, Oreg.: Multnomah, 1991), 118; cited in DeMoss, *Learn to Discern,* 26.
5. James Dobson, *Hide or Seek* (Old Tappan, N.J.: Revell, 1974), 12.
6. Ibid., 17.
7. Bill Gothard, *Self-acceptance,* Institute in Basic Youth Conflicts, October 1984, 4–6.
8. Dobson, *Hide or Seek,* 51.
9. Tim Hansel, *What Kids Need Most in a Dad* (Tarrytown, N.Y.: Revell, 1989), 75.

WHEN YOU JUDGE NEOPAGANISM

When Does Fantasy Become Reality?

For the most part, Christians in America no longer fear the devil.

There was a time when people understood that the devil actually existed and could not be trusted to play by the rules. But today, although Christians nod an awareness of Satan and his hordes, they actually think that they can enter his turf without any reprisals. They believe that the devil is gentleman enough to stay away unless he is invited to the party.

Why are Christians, for the most part, not afraid of the occult?

First, they wrongly think that if an occult object, game, or story is accepted as fantasy, then it is not to be feared. As long as one does not believe in the power of a Ouija board, then it is not dangerous. As long as one reads horoscopes for fun, there is nothing wrong with the practice. Or if

Dungeons and Dragons is thought of as just an innocent game, it is not occult. The world of Harry Potter is harmless, if it is seen as imaginary.

But I must warn that fantasy can very quickly turn into reality. Fantasy is the bridge that often leads to the other side of the spiritual world. We can't expect that we are exempt from satanic attack just because we accept the occult as fantasy.

> IT IS BETTER TO WARN AGAINST DANGER THAN TO FLIRT WITH IT.

Second, some Christians think they would know whether or not the devil was present in an experience. If they don't see him or feel him, if a dark presence does not enter the room, they think they are safe from his advances. They do not understand that the devil comes under different disguises. They forget that he often stays hidden as long as possible and that we can encounter him when we are only playing a "harmless" occult game or committing a favorite sin.

Third, there is the widespread assumption that if we find someone who has not been hurt by involvement in a specific aspect of the occult, this proves it is not really dangerous. So we hear, "I know someone who went to a fortune teller and it didn't hurt him," or, "I know someone who played with a Ouija board and nothing happened."

I've known several people who have seen the movie *The Exorcist*. Some, apparently, were not adversely affected; but at least one person I knew encountered a demon that needed to be exorcised. Some have been into astrology without adverse effects; but others have found themselves bound to satanic powers as a result of their participation. If you ask, "Why do occult practices affect one person and not another?"

I cannot answer. Why do some people get food poisoning in a restaurant, while others who ordered the same menu have no ill effects?

My point is simply this: An activity cannot be classified as harmless just because some people have no apparent bad effects. I say *apparent*, because none of us know what the long-term consequences might be. Often involvement in the occult does not involve overt possession, but it paralyzes spiritual growth, and the Christian finds it difficult (some would say impossible) to read the Bible or pray because of satanic opposition.

Some parents think that if we guide our children properly, they should be ready to see or read anything, just as long as we help them separate the true from the false. That is correct, of course, to a point. But what parents forget is that any level of occult involvement can sow seeds that bear bitter fruit in the years to come.

A mother whose husband plays *Dungeons and Dragons* with their ten-year-old son writes, "I think you will find many who disagree with the categorical distinction of *Dungeons and Dragons* being occult. It has been perverted by providing people with the opportunity to escape their real lives and responsibilities, but we communicate with our child to keep him from danger." She goes on to say that, in their case, the game is led by a Christian student. Then she adds, "I agree that gaming can be obsessive and addictive . . . that is why my husband and I are so involved with our ten-year-old son in this matter." I commend these parents for communicating with their son, but I think it is unwise to introduce him to any game that has the power to become occult. It is better to warn against danger than to flirt with it.

Fourth, some Christians believe that they have special protection from Satan. I heard a young Roman Catholic girl say that she could attend occult movies as long as she was "in a state of grace" and that she had spiritual protection from demonic invasion. Protestants have our own rationale; we think we are protected because we are "in Christ." This, it is believed, exempts us from anything but the mildest of demonic attacks.

Let us never underestimate the extent to which God lets

> THE OCCULT IS A FORM OF SELF-EMPOWERMENT.

Satan attack and harass believers who toy with what He (God) condemns! Whether or not we believe that Christians can be demon possessed, they most assuredly can be bound and oppressed by our Enemy.

Finally, there is the supposition that if some immediate good comes from the occult practice, this means it must be good. We might know someone who was able to lose weight or quit smoking by the use of hypnotism, and therefore some think it is a legitimate practice. No matter that the Bible condemns charmers and enchanters (biblical terms for hypnotism). We should fear hypnotism even if it is done by a Christian.

Satan comes uninvited; he appears in many different ways and under different guises. When Judas was contemplating betraying Christ, we read, "Satan entered into him" (John 13:27). Satan entered into Judas when he was sitting at the table in the Upper Room next to Jesus! Judas had not yet committed his great sin; he was only thinking about it. No formal invitation was needed for Satan to enter; all Judas needed to do was to contemplate a sin in his heart—admittedly a great sin—and Satan entered into him without warning and without fanfare.

Satan wants us to develop confidence in our ability to toy with his lures; he wants us to think that because he does not strike *every* time, he can be trusted to not strike at *any* time. But we have every reason to fear when we enter his territory.

GOD'S OPINION OF THE OCCULT

God is not neutral regarding occult involvement.

When you enter the land the LORD your God is giving you, do not learn to imitate the detestable ways of the nations there. Let no one be found among you who sacrifices his son or daughter in the fire, who practices divination or sorcery, interprets omens, engages in witchcraft, or casts spells, or who is a medium or spiritist or who consults the dead. Anyone who does these things is detestable to the LORD, and because of these detestable practices the LORD your God will drive out those nations before you. You must be blameless before the LORD your God. (Deuteronomy 18:9–13)

The Bible lists some twenty different occult practices. Here we have just a few:

- *Divination*—foreseeing the future or knowing certain facts about people that could only be known by spiritual revelation
- *Sorcery*—magic with the aid of evil spirits
- *Omens*—objects or events that predict good or bad fortune

- *Witchcraft*—power in the spirit world
- *Spells*—words with magical powers, such as incantations and the like
- *Mediums*—people who try to communicate with the dead
- *Spiritualists*—people who also purport to be in contact with the dead and who have a wide range of occult interests

The occult has several characteristics that pique our curiosity. It taps into our desire to be in touch with something greater than ourselves; it entices us to experience something beyond the mundane world of human existence, and as such it becomes a substitute for God.

Why does God hate these practices?

First, the occult holds out the promise of hidden knowledge that can't be gathered by scientific analysis; it invites us to have information that lies beyond our observation. Notice the list: divination, sorcery, interpretation of omens, witchcraft, consulting the dead. People want to peer into the future; they want to decipher the meaning of life. They want to know things that God has not chosen to reveal.

Second, the occult promises power that God has not authorized. There is power to cast spells, to manipulate events, to control the outcome of circumstances. Occultists want special powers to "even the score" and thereby wrest justice from God's hand and put it into their own. There are many who think that the occult is morally neutral; it can be used for either good things or bad things, depending on the person who has these awesome powers.

The bottom line: The occult is a form of self-empowerment;

it is the means by which we turn from God to ourselves to find meaning and significance in life. A worshiper of Satan said, "Actually, we don't worship Satan; we worship ourselves and nature and Satan just shows up."

God calls these practices detestable, and it was because of these things that the pagan nations were destroyed. It might well be that because of these practices, America will also be destroyed.

DOORWAYS TO THE OCCULT

Let me list some ways that the occult comes to us.

New Age Healing

Any practice or object that claims supernatural power to heal (either physically or emotionally) is also a substitute for faith in the one true God. Crystals and psychic therapies that use "healing guides" make such claims. Millions of Americans are now combining nutrition and psychic or spiritual experiences to create a "holistic" approach to health. This fad tries to combine the mind sciences with physical science to achieve a sense of well-being. Teachings derived from Eastern philosophies are deftly mixed with legitimate information on good health. Thus we have lectures on reflexology, visualization, and self-hypnosis.

I've collected brochures featuring some of the seminars available, such as *Awakening the Healer Within: A Practitioner's Introduction to Therapeutic Touch;* then there is *Psychoimmunity and the Healing Process,* which promises that we can unite our mind and body and "we will access our own innate abilities to achieve health and balance in our lives." The list is endless.

Best-selling author Deepak Chopra, whose books have been translated into twenty-five languages, teaches that the basic substance of our bodies isn't matter, but energy and information. True health results from a balanced flow of this energy throughout the body. Maintaining this energy balance necessitates things like herbs, gemstones, personality typing, and *yagyas* (religious ceremonies to solicit the aid of Hindu deities).[1]

Of course we all agree that the mind has a great influence over the body because the two work together in ways we do not fully understand. The error of "holistic health" is that the mind is given supernatural powers; the assumption is that *you can be your own healer because you can be your own god.* One devotee claimed that "unseen doctors are working through me." The witch doctor is back, but this time he holds expensive seminars and has a "scientific" explanation for his occult powers.

Psychedelic Drugs and Transcendental Meditation

On the surface, practices such as transcendental meditation appear harmless. What could possibly be wrong with spending time trying to empty the mind of all pressures of life and just think about *nothing?* Combine that with exercise that demands concentration, and your blood pressure is sure to drop and your finely tuned body will feel much better.

But transcendental meditation is based on the religious conviction that the soul must be united with the one unified force of the universe. Rationality is seen as the hindrance to this oneness and mystical unity with God. As long as I am thinking about *something,* I perceive myself to be distinct from the objects of this world. Thus, I must empty my mind of specific thoughts and try to think of a contentless reality. S. N. Dasgupta writes that the yogi "steadily proceeds toward that ultimate state in which his mind will be disintegrated and his self will shine forth in its own light and he himself will be absolutely free in bondless, companionless loneliness of self-illumination."[2]

At some point, the participant experiences a conversion experience called *enlightenment.* This mystical experience enables one to go beyond personality, beyond morality, beyond knowledge. The conversion Satan has wrought is complete—the transformation of consciousness has occurred. But with demonic spirits influencing the mind, there is a cloud of darkness rather than enlightenment that enters the soul. This deception can only be uncovered in honest contemplation in the presence of God, Bible in hand.

Psychedelic drugs can achieve the same transformation. When the mind is opened to whatever powers there be, demonic spirits in the atmosphere are delighted to enter to deceive and control. This explains why those who are in the drug culture often need specific deliverance from dark, occult powers.

Television Programs and Movies

Doorways into the occult exist everywhere, but television and movies cast the widest net and capture the greatest number of recruits. Television shows such as *Buffy the Vampire*

Slayer and *Charmed* and movies such as *Practical Magic* and *The Craft* make the occult popular. Many people attend these movies or watch these television programs and think they are harmless and cute. But they are loaded with occult messages and lures.

In an article titled "Weird Sisters," Margaret Kim Peterson explains how these shows portray witchcraft as a kind of pantheistic nature religion. Witches in the movie *The Craft* announce, "We worship everything; God, the devil, the earth, trees."[3] One of the witches in *Practical Magic* explains that witchcraft has to do with being close to nature. Witchcraft is accompanied by many accessories: candles, occult symbols, brooms, potions, books on how to cast spells. These young witches evoke the power of the wind or the power of the trees.

> OUR ENEMY DOES HIS MOST DARING WORK WHEN WE ARE ALONE, INWARD FOCUSED, AND CURIOUS ABOUT THE DARKNESS.

What do witches get in exchange for these charms? They have a variety of paranormal powers, such as levitation, psychic power to see the future, and the ability to manipulate the thoughts of others or to destroy certain kinds of evil. Sometimes they have to defend themselves against an occult power that has gone wrong.

There is a downside to being a witch. Sometimes these powers are hard to control; witches are often misunderstood and rejected. So they have to conceal and lie about their vocation. And yet, it is not easy to opt out of being a witch, because certain people are born into it. Some grow up and only later discover that they were born to be witches.

What is important is that they accept their differences, for as Peterson points out, "Not accepting yourself is the original sin in these media tales of witchcraft."

From these shows we learn that witchcraft is passed from mother to daughter. As one of the sisters in *Charmed* notes, "It's a chick thing—it's passed down the female line." Thus these witches discover that their mothers were witches before them. The bonds of witchcraft are passed along through blood rituals, and they are often banded together by a curse. Thus they are called upon to exorcise demons, though they are both glad and apprehensive about doing so.

These witches have all experienced abuse at the hands of men. They desire the love of a man, but they are deeply afraid that men will abuse them or abandon them. Thus their relationship with men turns seductive and murderously angry. They are filled with revenge for the evil that men have done to them. The sisters in *Charmed* were abandoned as children by their father. They all behave seductively toward men, but their relationships are always abusive; the witches must protect themselves, for the men always try to take advantage of them.

The sisters in *Practical Magic* come from a long line of witches who live under a curse pronounced by a foremother who was abandoned by her lover. The curse stipulates that any man they love will die an untimely death. When one sister falls in love, it is with a man who beats her and tries to murder her. "It takes an entire coven to vanquish this man once and for all, and when he has been finally destroyed, one of the witches turns to the other and says, 'I wonder if that would work on my ex-husband.'"[4]

What is the theology of these shows? Peterson points

out that God is one of several comparable spiritual entities; He is there along with nature, or perhaps as being one with nature. No one is ultimately in charge of what happens in the world. As a woman who runs a witchcraft supply store in *The Craft* explains, "Magic is neither good nor bad; it is both, because nature is both." The spiritual dimensions are presented as powerful, but if a person is careful and has good intentions, he can use it in sort of a way for that which is good. "There is no sense that any spiritual entity might be either so evil or so holy that it would be foolhardy to have anything to do with it."[5]

"In such a scenario," writes Peterson, "it is not surprising that redemption is missing. In all of these shows, the good people do not need to be redeemed and the bad people cannot be." So the good need simply to be rewarded, the evil people punished. There is no forgiveness, no grace, and no possibility of change."[6]

Perhaps we can better understand why these movies are so appealing. Many young women can identify with having been abused or at least misused by men. Since men are going to abandon you, the reasoning goes, the only lasting relationship can come through friendship with women. What is more, becoming a witch with the power to cast spells and wreak havoc is an inviting way to get back at the male species. Human justice says that they are getting what they deserve.

At a time when our homes are in disarray and men do abuse women, it is easy to see why these shows touch an emotional cord. Just think of how enticing all of this might be to abused teenagers who feel that they must protect themselves from the hurts of this world by connecting to some power that is greater than themselves.

Peterson concludes, "Far from challenging human devotion to consumerism, sex, violence, and individual fulfillment, witchcraft is just one more way of having just what one wants, and having it now."[7] Anton LaVey, founder of the church of Satan said, "This is a very selfish religion. We believe in greed, we believe in selfishness, we believe in all of the lustful thoughts that motivate man, because this is man's natural feeling."[8]

Just surf your television channels if you have any doubt that movies are laced with occult rituals and references. Millions of teenagers, along with many adults, find themselves intrigued, curious, and finally drawn into some kind of involvement. Satan plays by no rules, so he will impose his darkness on anyone who comes near his realm. Telltale signs of those affected are mood swings, morbid introspection, and isolation from others. Our Enemy does his most daring work when we are alone, inward focused, and curious about the darkness. And the more we dabble in his playpen, the more helpless we are of turning back.

Astrology

The Tower of Babel was destroyed because of astrology; God was angry with the people when they turned to the stars to read their fortunes and futures. But that did not end man's fascination with this occultic practice. Centuries later, God angrily taunted the Babylonians for their reliance on astrology.

Keep on, then, with your magic spells
      and with your many sorceries,
         which you have labored at since childhood.
Perhaps you will succeed,
      perhaps you will cause terror.
All the counsel you have received has only worn you out!
      Let your astrologers come forward,
those stargazers who make predictions month by month,
      let them save you from what is coming upon you.
Surely they are like stubble;
      the fire will burn them up.
They cannot even save themselves
      from the power of the flame. . . .
Each of them goes on in his error;
      there is not one that can save you.
                                    (Isaiah 47:12–14, 15b)

Just dial this number for a free psychic hotline reading!
We've all heard and seen the ads on television that invite
tarot readings. What follows are personal testimonies of
people whose lives were changed because they spoke to
someone who could foresee their fortunes and misfortunes,
their impending romances, and their vocational opportunities. And, thanks to human ingenuity, they were able to take
advantage of the hidden knowledge.

Of course, sometimes these "prophets" get it right. If
you make enough predictions you will not be wrong every
time. Some of these psychics can see into the future as far as
the devil can; others are just charlatans. Whatever, God is
not amused.

Astrology is an abomination because it bypasses God in

the search for wisdom; in effect, it is shaking one's fist in the face of the Almighty. Ouija boards, horoscopes, fortune-tellers and other such practices violate this basic principle. They are appealing snares that lead the unwary into submission to occult phenomena controlled by the Enemy.

To Potter or Not to Potter?

What about the fantasy series *Harry Potter?* These fiction novels by J. K. Rowling are said to represent the "greatest triumph in publishing history." Some Christians who initially opposed the books changed their minds after they read the series. The argument is that it is possible for a writer to use occult themes as a literary device without promoting the occult as such. Certainly Tolkien and C. S. Lewis have done so.

> THERE ARE ONLY TWO SOURCES OF SPIRITUAL POWER; THERE IS GOD AND THERE IS SATAN.

Some Christians insist that the witchcraft in *Harry Potter* is purely mechanical; that is, it is used to create a story and make a point. I fear, however, that *Harry Potter* could easily become what Mark Filiatreau called an "imaginative bridge" connecting children to the dangerous world of the occult.[9]

Perhaps the *Harry Potter* series is a matter of individual conscience, yet my own quick survey of the material finds that book four is especially dark and violent. Given that witchcraft is presented with a "friendly face" throughout, I find it difficult to see how these stories could be beneficial for children.

I offer some questions that might be helpful in evaluating the material; I believe that these questions will also help distinguish Harry Potter from the writings of Tolkien and C. S. Lewis.

- Does the fantasy teach absolutes, or is it based on relativistic notions of good and evil?
- Is evil presented as "good" in the stories?
- Are spells, curses, and various "evil powers" used for vengeance?
- Does reading the book make the reader feel more at home with the occult or more afraid of it?
- Is it possible to break the rules and still be a hero?
- After reading the book or seeing the movie, would children be more inclined or less inclined to seek hidden powers and secret knowledge?

For a biblical, in-depth evaluation of the *Harry Potter* books, see Richard Abanes's *Harry Potter and the Bible*.[10]

> THE OCCULT IS EVIL, EVEN WHEN IT APPEARS TO BE GOOD.

Warning flags must be heeded. It is dangerous to introduce children to the world of the occult.

A word to parents: If your children have read these books, or are insistent on doing so, read the books with them and point out the differences between the worldview of Harry Potter and the Christian worldview. Help them to understand that this is a story that employs practices that the Bible condemns. Better yet, give them other kinds of fiction that present a distinctively Christian worldview.

Principles of Discernment

How can we exercise discernment in this world filled with occultism and undefined spirituality? Because these powers are invisible, we need some principles to guide us.

Two Sources of Spiritual Power

We've already learned that there are only two sources of spiritual power; there is God and there is Satan. There is no neutral power of "nature" or "mother earth"; we must not think that we must harness the "power of mind." All supernatural power (that is, power above the natural) is derived from one of two sources. Whatever is not based on God and the Bible is occultic and sinful.

The distinction often made between harmful "black magic" and good "white magic" is bogus. Think this through: If you were the devil, would you not let people use your powers for good purposes if you knew that thereby you could deceive them and grasp them more tightly later on? Yes, you would. You'd give them something good if later you could give them something bad. We must remember that the occult is evil, even when it appears to be good.

Many years ago, I was on a television program with a witch, a member of Wicca, and she insisted that the witches have nothing to do with the devil. They just tap the powers of "nature" and they are committed to do good things with these powers, she said.

To be fair we must point out that not all witches directly worship Satan. Some are opposed to animal sacrifices because they see everything in nature as divine. Yes, there are witches who attempt to be in harmony with nature, developing their hidden psychic power. But whether Satan is worshiped directly or under the guise of nature, the end result is essentially the same. There are only two personal spiritual powers in the universe, God and the devil. *Satan can be worshiped even when he is not named.*

Small Steps, Big Gains

Even small steps, if going in the wrong direction, can eventually lead into Satan's trap. Because we are curious about the occult, we must guard our hearts, our minds, and our homes. Evil has fascination; the occult can appeal to our lower natures, just as immorality does. That is why Paul lists witchcraft as a work of the flesh (Galatians 5:20).

> IT IS ALWAYS EASIER TO DEFEND TERRITORY THAN TO WIN IT BACK AFTER IT HAS BEEN CONCEDED TO THE ENEMY.

Three men were interviewed for becoming a truck driver. The same question was asked each of them: How close could you come to the edge of a cliff while driving? One said, "I could come within six inches." Another said, "I could come as close as four inches." A third said, "I can only tell you I would stay as far away from the edge as possible." He got the job.

We should not be asking how close it is possible for us to come to the occult without giving Satan a right to our lives, but rather, how far we can stay away from his domain. We must not read any book or see any movie that "messes with our mind," as the saying goes. The reason is that the mind is a spiritual substance that can either be in touch with God or with the devil. Any technique that seeks to "empty the mind" is dangerous, for evil spirits lurk about, waiting for an opportunity to bring deception and havoc.

A Reward in Exchange for Control

Satan will give you what you want as long as you eventually get what he wants. He will heal your body; he will bring you money; he will prosper your vocation, as long as the noose is tied a bit tighter. He will help you lose weight through hypnotism; he will bring you good luck through a fortune teller; he will do all that and more if, in return, he can entice you to have an "addictive allegiance" to sin.

He wants us to think that we can have it all. You can keep your money, pursue your pleasures, and satisfy your ego. You can accept the notion that whatever the mind can believe, the mind can achieve. In exchange for success on such premises, there will be an eventual payback. In the end, our lives are wasted, our witness paralyzed, and our relationship with God tarnished. Satan lets us appear to win today so that he can exercise more control tomorrow.

Ignorance Is No Excuse

Just because someone does not know that attempting levitation, playing with tarot cards, or consulting a witch is wrong does not exempt him from satanic harassment. Suppose you were an Israeli soldier and decided to take a walk on a sunny afternoon, and, without knowing it, you crossed the border into Lebanon. It would do little good to protest that this was not your fault since there were no border markings. Don't expect the Lebanese to say, "Oh, well, yes, the border was not marked as well as it should have been, so we'll let you return."

The devil does not play by the rules. He cannot be trusted to maintain reasonable boundaries. Since he lacks compassion, he does not give us a pass for ignorance. Often there is no second chance; most assuredly there is no grace, no opportunity to retrace our steps. When we cross into his domain, we can expect the hassle of our lives.

> GETTING FREE FROM SATANIC POWER IS NOT JUST A ONCE-FOR-ALL ACT, BUT RATHER A LIFESTYLE.

Warning: *Let us never forget that the best defense against the occult is to refuse every invitation to become involved in its many overtures.* Ask any army general and he will tell you that it is always easier to defend territory than to win it back after it has been conceded to the enemy. Those of us who have children must warn them of the danger of dabbling in what God has specifically forbidden. Sin, we must remember, is always our enemy, never our friend.

Christ Has Triumphed

God raised Jesus from the dead and "seated him at his right hand in the heavenly realms, far above all rule and authority, power and dominion, and every title that can be given, not only in the present age but also in the one to come" (Ephesians 1:20–21). Satan's greatest fear is that we will understand that he is defeated and that God has made it possible for us to be wrenched free of his grip. He fears detection and bold confrontation.

Of course, there is hope for those who have been involved in some aspect of occult activity. Yes, Satan might retaliate as you seek to be free of occult activity, but you can be free if you are absolutely convinced of the triumph of Christ over the kingdom of darkness.

Keep in mind that on the cross Christ won a decisive victory; the serpent has already been crushed.

He forgave us all our sins, having canceled the written code, with its regulations, that was against us and that stood opposed to us; he took it away, nailing it to the cross. And having disarmed the powers and authorities, he made a public spectacle of them, triumphing over them by the cross. (Colossians 2:13–15)

Only when looking at Christ will we not be intimidated, for *Satan has as much power as God lets him have and not one whit more.*

I must clarify that getting free from satanic power is not just a once-for-all act but rather a lifestyle. One act of renunciation, one decisive moment of repentance is not sufficient. Depending on the level and kind of involvement, it is possible that you need counseling to help you break the bonds that hold you to the dark side of the spirit world.

At Moody Church, where I serve, a minister gave a powerful message on the occult and listed forty different entry points or practices that lead to such enslavement. That evening, he invited all those who had some form of involvement and wanted freedom to stay behind for counsel. About thirty-five people stayed for counsel, and, incredibly, forty of the occult practices were represented (many of the people were, of course, involved in more than one form of occult activity).

Burn all bridges that led you into the occult. You must be held accountable to stay away from all people and places that led you into occult sin. This is more difficult than it seems, particularly if you live with those who are prone to influence you to return to the pagan practices. We have this promise, "Submit therefore to God. Resist the devil and he will flee from you" (James 4:7 NASB). There is great power in the name of Christ but only for those who are submissive to His authority.

> JUST BECAUSE THIS WAR IS INVISIBLE DOESN'T MEAN IT ISN'T REAL.

Repent of this involvement, asking God to break the ties that still bind. For example a prayer might be, "Father, I thank You that I belong to You; You have 'translated me from the kingdom of darkness, into the kingdom of Your dear Son,' and I claim that transfer of authority and privilege. I renounce my involvement in _____ and break all ties to this evil. I affirm that I am 'in Christ' and therefore no longer subject to Satan and his kingdom. Today I thank You for the victory Christ purchased for me. I affirm the power of the Cross and the Resurrection as belonging to me."

Just because this war is invisible doesn't mean it isn't real. It does mean that we have to know our adversary and our weapons and fight accordingly. "You, dear children, are from God and have overcome them, because the one who is in you is greater than the one who is in the world" (1 John 4:4). Thanks to Jesus, we are on the winning side.

NOTES

Portions of this chapter first appeared in *Seven Snares of the Enemy: Breaking Free from the Devil's Grip,* by Erwin W. Lutzer (Chicago: Moody, 2001).

1. Dónal P. O'Mathúna,"Postmodern Impact: Healthcare," cited in Dennis Mc-Callum, ed., *The Death of Truth* (Minneapolis: Bethany House, 1996), 60.
2. S. N. Dasgupta, *Hindu Mysticism* (New York: Frederick Unger, 1927), 79.
3. Margaret Kim Peterson, "Weird Sisters," *Books and Culture: A Christian Review,* March/April 1999, 24.
4. Ibid., 25.
5. Ibid.
6. Ibid.
7. Ibid.
8. Anton LaVey, cited in John Ankerberg and John Weldon, *The Coming Darkness* (Eugene, Ore.: Harvest House, 1993), 94.
9. Mark Filiatreau, "Pokémon, Harry Potter, and the Magic of Story," Breakpoint Online, Prison Fellowship Ministry; accessed at www.breakpoint.org and www.christianity.com.
10. Richard Abanes, *Harry Potter and the Bible* (Camp Hill, Pa.: Horizon, 2001). I recommend this book to those who would want a balanced, biblical evaluation of the *Harry Potter* series.

9

WHEN YOU JUDGE GHOSTS, ANGELS, AND SHRINES

How Shall We Interpret the Spirit World?

About once a year, usually around Halloween, the *Chicago Tribune* gives a list and description of the haunted houses of Chicago. And, yes, there are haunted restaurants and haunted apartments. Some are famous; others are just regular rooms that have disembodied spirits. I've spoken to people who tell stories about the "old man who lived upstairs" or of a grandmother who died in the past decade but makes regular visits. Indeed, there are "ghost hunters" who claim that they can detect the presence of these strange creatures.

Several years ago the *Calgary Herald* reported that a hotel in the area was haunted; at least two rooms were inhabited with unseen visitors who made their presence known to the guests. Interestingly, the very week the story was in the news, I was booked in the hotel for a conference.

When the opportunity came for us to take a tour of the hotel, a number of us accepted the offer. We were shown the beautiful woodwork, the expensive fixtures, and rugs from as far away as England. We were also taken to the downstairs cafeteria where there was a stairwell covered with potted plants.

"This stairwell," said our guide, "is not used because the stairs are haunted." She went on to say that when the first wedding took place in the hotel, the bride fell down the stairs and died, and now her ghost appears. In fact, we could ask the people who work in the cafeteria and they would verify that the young woman appeared from time to time.

How do we explain this phenomenon? Recall that when Jesus cast the demons out of the demented man, they requested permission to enter the swine, and Jesus granted their request (Mark 5:13). When a person who is inhabited by an evil spirit dies, this spirit needs to relocate. This seems particularly true in the case of a violent death, such as murder or suicide. These spirits will take the name and imitate the characteristics of the deceased and make occasional appearances under those pretenses. Such entities (as they are frequently called today) are evil spirits who often pose as "friendly ghosts."

> A WRONG VIEW OF MAN LEADS TO A WRONG VIEW OF GOD.

This explains why mediums who contact the dead are actually speaking to evil spirits who impersonate the deceased. Understandably, the Bible calls these spirits *familiar* spirits, because they are familiar with the person whom they have adopted (Leviticus 19:31; 20:6, 27; Deuteronomy 18:11; 1 Samuel 28:7, all KJV). Thus the medium is deceived into thinking that communication has actually taken place with the dead, not knowing that he or she has encountered a spirit who only knew the dead. Incredibly, a television show titled *Crossing Over* now ensnares millions with the mistaken idea that contact has been achieved because the medium does in fact conjure up information that was true about the deceased. Relatives rest with the false hope that their loved one is trying to tell them that he is doing fine, when in fact that loved one might actually be suffering in hades (Luke 16:19–31).

The point, of course, is that all information about life after death that comes from spiritists or channelers is unreliable. Those who turn to the occult world for knowledge of life after death or to communicate with the departed are misled. Yes, there is life after death, but we cannot learn the details from demons whose chief delight is to confuse and deceive.

That day in Calgary, I asked the guide if she would want a biblical explanation for this phenomenon of "ghosts." I told her that the spirit of the woman was not on those stairs but had gone on to another world, but that spirits—yes, evil spirits—who had been acquainted with the living often stay in the vicinity of the death.

She said that she preferred the word *ghost* rather than spirit—like Casper, the friendly ghost. But if ghosts are spirits from the dark side of the spirit world, no ghost should be considered harmless, even if it appears friendly. These spirits must be rebuked in the name of our risen Savior.

THE RISE OF ANGELS

Today we have television programs dedicated to miracles, to angels, and to spirituality of every kind. The basic

formula of the television show *Touched by an Angel*, as stated
by the producers, is this: "The angel meets her assigned human at a crossroads in his or her life. The angel (by the power of God) performs a miracle to bring that person to a point
of decision or revelation. He or she, by their own free will,
then takes life-changing action."[1]

Thus, in virtually every episode, a troubled person is
helped; perhaps there is a physical healing or an emotional
barrier is overcome. Sometimes the needy person might be
facing a personal crisis in his or her marriage or with the
children. Whatever, an angel is used by God to resolve the crisis, proving that there is a spiritual dimension to the world
and that the Almighty stands at the ready to help us by
sending angels to those who least deserve or expect it. Each
show has a feel-good ending, since a crisis has been resolved and the troubled person has turned a corner, setting
out in a new direction.

Why do I object to this harmless story line?

These stories are loaded with theology, a cultural theology that reinforces prevalent views about man and God.
Through its pleasing portrayals of needy people helped by
heavenly messengers, these notions lob a grenade at the
heart of the Christian gospel.

These angel stories assume that people are basically
good, rather than sinners who stand in desperate need of
God's saving grace. This reinforces the prevailing myth that
sin is not our problem, but that we must simply overcome a
feeling of disconnectedness, a need to know how God's help
can be enlisted. Thankfully, an angel comes to help in a crisis, and there is relief in knowing that at last one has made
contact with God.

Since a wrong view of man leads to a wrong view of God, we should not be surprised that the God presented by modern culture is one that can be accessed by anyone, at any time, and in any way. Like Cain, who thought God could be approached in whatever creative way he selected, popular culture teaches that ordinary people, if they have enough ordinary good will, can have contact with God without a mediator, without a sacrifice, and without blood.

"But," you protest, "these shows do not claim to be specifically Christian but are committed to presenting a generic faith, showing that there are people who believe in God and that angels are real beings, just as the Bible says." But the point cannot be made too strongly that these assumptions reinforce a destructive cultural stereotype.

What do we make of the angel stories, the reports of angels intervening to help people?

We can't always tell the difference between good and bad angels. The evil angels are willing to make as many concessions as possible to deceive the unwary. The angels of darkness turn themselves into angels of light so that people will be confused about their real identity.

1. *Evil angels are willing to mouth solid, evangelical doctrine.* When Christ was in the synagogue in Capernaum He met a man with an unclean spirit, who, when confronted by Christ, cried out, "What do you want with us, Jesus of Nazareth? Have you come to destroy us? I know who you are—the Holy One of God!" (Mark 1:24).

What is more, demons confessed that Christ was the Son of God. "What do you want with me, Jesus, Son of the Most High God? Swear to God that you won't torture me!"

(Mark 5:7). These are the words of a demon responding to Christ's command to leave the demented man. These demons could, in effect, sign an evangelical statement of faith that affirmed that Christ was "The Holy One of God" or "The Son of the Most High God."

Of course demons do not make such admissions willingly or gladly. But when in the presence of Christ, or when attempting to deceive, they will confess correct doctrine. Yes, they are capable of appearing and quoting, "Hear, O Israel: The LORD our God, the LORD is one" (Deuteronomy 6:4) if the words will deceive one of their victims.

2. *Evil angels will, if possible, duplicate the miracles of Christ.* Paul warned that Satan would come with "counterfeit miracles, signs and wonders" (2 Thessalonians 2:9). Evil angels will do helpful miracles if they can and if it serves their long-term goals, namely, diverting people from the purity of the gospel of Christ.

A man who was healed from a serious disease in a so-called healing meeting discovered that he had also inherited a "demonic darkness," that is, a persistent sense that he now had an evil presence near him. When he rebuked Satan, the emotional and spiritual cloud left him but his disease returned. We should not be surprised that healings occur in all the religions of the world. Satan is willing to give something that appears good in exchange for blind allegiance.

Thus, it is not possible for us to always distinguish the good from the bad. It is simply not wise to navigate the metaphysical landscape without a map, a guide that lets us call these angelic beings by their correct designation.

3. Evil angels have all of the essential powers of good angels. As far as we know, evil angels can perform many assignments for Satan that are similar to those done by God's angels. Think of the awesome "victory" (albeit temporary) Satan wins when millions of people mistake his intervention as the intervention of God and His angels!

Remember, Satan's goal is not to create as much misery as he

> UNLESS SPIRITUALITY IS BASED ON THE AUTHORITY OF THE BIBLE, IT WILL ALWAYS SPAWN SUPERSTITIONS AND A GULLIBLE GENERATION.

can on planet earth; he wants to make us comfortable while keeping his eventual goals in sight. His primary objective is to spread false doctrine, to reinforce the cultural conception of God. He wants people to believe in a benevolent God who dispenses help to all. It is naive to say, as some do, that reported miracles must be the work of good angels because the effects are good and beneficial. We must boldly say that "good" miracles can be done by "bad" angels.

TELLING THE DIFFERENCE

So the question is: How do we interpret the dramatic rescues, healings, and help given to people who are in desperate straits? What do we say about the accounts of "divine interventions" of heavenly beings that make everything turn out just right, regardless of what people believe about Christ? Think through the following:

1. God's good angels are given assignments limited to the people of God. They are not sent indiscriminately to all men and women. "Are not all angels ministering spirits sent to serve those who will inherit salvation?" (Hebrews 1:14). Thus, we have the function of angels defined for us in Scripture. If angels are ever sent to help those who have not accepted Christ and therefore "will not inherit salvation," we have no account of it in Scripture.

2. *God's good angels participate in acts of judgment for the unconverted.* Yes, angels are sometimes sent to the unconverted, but only to judge them. We think immediately of the angels who visited with Abraham and had the responsibility of executing judgment on Sodom and Gomorrah. Angels did help Lot escape the city, but only because he was a believer in Jehovah and therefore a "righteous man" (2 Peter 2:7).

Repeatedly, in the book of Revelation, angels are directly involved in executing judgment on those who have not come under the protection of Christ's sacrifice. For example, in chapter 14 a succession of angels comes announcing judgment. One warns that if anyone worships the beast "he, too, will drink of the wine of God's fury, which has been poured full strength into the cup of his wrath. He will be tormented with burning sulfur in the presence of the holy angels and of the Lamb" (Revelation 14:10). The angel that followed announced the impending judgment, and the next angel executed it.

Read carefully: "Still another angel, who had charge of the fire, came from the altar and called in a loud voice to him who had the sharp sickle, 'Take your sharp sickle and gather the clusters of grapes from the earth's vine, because its grapes are ripe'" (v. 18). Then notice what this angel does.

"The angel swung his sickle on the earth, gathered its grapes and threw them into the great winepress of God's wrath" (v. 19). Later in the book, an angel invites the birds in midheaven to eat the flesh of kings, generals, and mighty men (19:17–18), now that God has destroyed them in judgment.

Needless to say, *Touched by an Angel* does not feature angels coming to execute the wicked. These Hollywood angels are always doing good deeds, even for people who might not be particularly religious; even for people who think of Christ as a teacher, not a Savior.

Unless spirituality is based on the authority of the Bible, it will always spawn superstitions and a gullible generation. We've all heard of Elvis sightings, and now that Princess Diana has become an international icon, I've heard that there are sightings of her too. The famous spiritist Emanuel Swedenborg recognized the difficulty of distinguishing good angels and bad. After years of spiritism, he wrote:

> When spirits begin to speak with a man, he ought to beware that he believes nothing whatever from them; for they say almost anything . . . they would tell so many lies, and indeed with solemn affirmation, that a man would be astonished . . . if a man listens and believes, they press on and deceive, and seduce in [many] ways.[2]

Elsewhere Paul warned, "But even if we or an angel from heaven should preach a gospel other than the one we preached to you, let him be eternally condemned!" (Galatians 1:8). Angels are not reliable as a source of revelation, simply because we might be listening to the wrong ones!

MIRACLES AT SHRINES

Perhaps you have heard the story that Mary appeared to a little country girl, Bernadette, in 1858 in Lourdes. "She was," said the girl, "a girl in white, no bigger than me." Mary had a gold and white rosary in her hands, and she smiled and said, "I am the Immaculate Conception." Interestingly, four years before this (1854), the Catholic Church officially accepted as dogma the "Immaculate Conception," that is, the view that Mary herself was born of a virgin and therefore without sin.

Back in 1990, Nancy Fowler, of Conyers, Georgia, claimed that Mary had visited her in her farm home about thirty miles east of Atlanta. "The future holds no concern to those who truly seek God and truly love him and remain in his favor," she told the crowd. For four years she delivered the same message on the thirteenth of each month. Then she announced that Mary would appear only once a year, on October 13. The crowd has steadily increased during the years, although she said that 1998 would be the last appearance of Mary on her farm. A hundred thousand people gathered as she read to them for some thirty minutes.[3]

These visions, it should be noted, were not endorsed by the local Catholic Church, yet people visited all the way from Mexico. Many claim they have either been healed or helped by meeting on this location. And even if the help is not directly evident, many who attended said they felt better, more in touch with their spiritual selves as a result of the visit.

What can we say about the miracles said to take place at Lourdes? Many who attend say that the experience enabled them to accept their own illness because they met people there who were worse off than they. And those who work at the shrine say that the people they meet and the opportunities for serving others change their perspective on what is truly valuable in life. Despite the obvious commercialism, many testify that the atmosphere is one of religious devotion, heartfelt friendships, and peace in the midst of the curious crowds.

Even the most devout observers admit that only a small percentage of the hundreds of thousands of sick who come to Lourdes experience healing of some kind. At least 90 percent of those seeking cures go away without benefit. (I'm sure the percentage is no different for Protestant faith healers.)

To the credit of the Catholic Church, miracles are not officially accepted without evidence. The Under Secretary at the Vatican's Congregation for the Causes of Saints investigates miracles because at least one or two are necessary in order for someone to be declared a saint. The theory is that a saint, after death, will be active on earth, answering prayers and persuading God to help sufferers below. Thus a committee consults with medical experts to determine whether indeed a miracle happened in response to petitions made in the name of the departed saint.

Interestingly, Mother Teresa, who died in 1997, was given a speedier route to sainthood because two miracles have been attributed to her. One reportedly happened in the United States, where a French woman broke several ribs in a car accident and was reportedly healed when she wore a Mother Teresa medallion around her neck. In the other miracle, a Palestinian girl suffering from cancer was apparently cured after Mother Teresa appeared in her dreams and said, "Child, you are healed."[4]

The International Medical Committee for the Shrine at Lourdes also evaluates evidence for miracles. Since all the miracles at the shrine are attributed to the intercession of Mary, this committee is not caught up in the saint-making process. According to *Time* magazine, no miracle has been approved since 1989. As medical science and psychology uncover rational explanations for more cures, it is increasingly difficult to name something a miracle.[5]

Of course, there may be cures of some sort that are not officially classified as miracles. French doctors often recommend a trip to Lourdes for those who are terminally ill, knowing that this is their last hope and that the faith that one will be healed has beneficial psychological effects. Even so, the number of disappointed people is beyond calculation. Of course, most who return home unhealed do not blame the Virgin but themselves: if only they had more faith; if only they had done more good deeds; if only they had been more faithful in praying the rosary. Whatever, the higher the hopes, the deeper the despair.

> THE BIBLE DOES NOT SANCTION MIRACLES PERFORMED BY JUST ANY PERSON OR ANY GOD.

To what do we ascribe the miracles that some say happened to them at Lourdes or other shrines? First, we cannot underestimate the power of suggestion. Those who make the trek believing they will be healed might find that their faith has helped them. Many ailments are psychosomatic; that is, they are either induced or perpetuated by the influence of the mind. Lourdes can change the disposition of the mind and therefore also the disposition of the body.

The miracles at Lourdes are much more akin to the healings reported by the Christian Scientist faith. I've browsed through books published by this religious group, reading one account of healing after another. But in most instances these miracles are those that can be explained psychologically; we cannot discount the power of the mind to overcome some of the maladies of the body.

Second, even if we admit that the number of miracles is much greater than those officially confirmed, many healings are incomplete. If we think that Mary performs these miracles instantly and completely, we are mistaken. When a physician wondered why the Virgin contented herself with healing a sore on the child's leg but not replacing the entire deformed foot, the answer given was that the scar on the leg remained as a testimony to the greatness of the miracle. Indeed, we are told that many miracles are partially accomplished so that the recipient remains in "grateful memory of the benefit received."[6]

In contrast, whenever Christ or the apostles performed a miracle in the New Testament, it was done completely and fully, instantly. It is inconceivable that God would intervene to heal a sore foot but leave the lacerated leg unhealed.

Third, at Lourdes everyone is invited to be healed, regardless of his doctrinal convictions, no matter what his devotion or his religion. At first blush this might seem as a plus; after all, Mary stands with arms open to all, without distinction. Indeed, the benefits of Mary are believed to be the common property of the whole world, regardless of one's religion or gods.[7] It is a message that dovetails with the tolerance of the day.

But wait.

If Mary has her arms open to all, regardless of the god

they worship, then we have no reason to think that these miracles are performed by God through Christ. The miracles in the New Testament were done by Jesus and by the apostles, who understood that Christ was the only way to God and that, therefore, these miracles were to be done "in His name." When Peter encountered Simon the Sorcerer, who "amazed all the people of Samaria" (Acts 8:9), Peter confronted him directly. Simon tried to buy the right to perform greater miracles—miracles of the caliber of Peter's— but Peter responded, "You have no part or share in this ministry, because your heart is not right before God. Repent of this wickedness and pray to the Lord. Perhaps he will forgive you for having such a thought in your heart. For I see that you are full of bitterness and captive to sin" (vv. 21–23). Proper doctrine and the right condition of your heart are essential if you want to perform miracles.

Let us not overlook the fact that when the Israelites worshiped the pagan goddess Ishtar, whom they called "the Queen of Heaven" (Jeremiah 7:18; 44:17–25), they insisted that it was she who gave them crops and food. In fact, they had the audacity to say, "But ever since we stopped burning incense to the Queen of Heaven and pouring out drink offerings to her, we have had nothing and have been perishing by sword and famine" (v. 18). *The Israelites were convinced that their prayers to a pagan goddess paid dividends; they thought they were better off because of their false worship.*

God would have none of it and told them that such worship was an abomination. But mark it well: It is possible to benefit from false worship; it is possible to claim miracles of provision and help. But even such "miracles" do not justify wrong doctrines. Remember that our only hope of interpreting a miracle correctly involves a careful study of the doctrinal context in which it is performed. Interestingly, this worship of Ishtar found its way into Christendom, and so it is that Mary has been called "The Queen of Heaven."

In his book *Expect a Miracle,* Dan Wakefield records that his search for miracles led him to many different shrines and many different religions. He discovered that every religion has its miracles. Buddhism has stories of "Tara healing people. . . . [In] times of despair you can call on her and she reaches out and comes to the rescue."[8] The Hindus have visions, encounters, rituals, and miracles. Wakefield quotes the *Washington Post* report that the power of prayer is gaining validity in helping the sick recover. Interestingly, regardless of the religion or deity, the beneficial effects are about the same.[9] Clearly, we need biblical discernment in this age of miracles.

The Bible does not sanction miracles performed by just any person or any god. To say that it does not matter what you believe is to say that it does not matter in whose name you are healed. We've already seen that even some who performed miracles in the name of Christ were excluded from heaven because they did not understand their need of redemption (Matthew 7:21–22). I must say it again: *Not everything that is miraculous is from God.*

On a plane I met a group of people en route to Europe to visit the various places where "Mary sightings" have occurred. They insisted that these sightings and their attendant miracles in no way detracted from the miracles of Christ. Let Christ do His miracles, and let His mother do hers.

But the matter is not that simple.

First, contrary to Catholic protests, this pursuit of the miraculous Mary sightings does detract from the miracles of Christ and the gospel. It is true, I think, that millions of people flock to the shrines of Mary with more hope, more anticipation, and more confidence than they have when they open their Bibles.

I have visited the shrine of Guadeloupe in Mexico and have seen crowds crawl on bleeding knees for hundreds of yards, approaching the shrine with the hope that they will win the favor of the Virgin Mary. Many are women with infants in their arms, hoping to appease her and enter into the sufferings of Christ. In Mexico, a form of Christianity blends nicely with pagan superstition and legends.

Perhaps the argument could be made that this is not actually Catholicism but rather a Catholicism that is mixed with pagan superstitions. Yet, interestingly, official Catholicism does not condemn these heretical beliefs and practices. Indeed, the Pope performed a mass at the shrine in 1999 without uttering a single word of rebuke for the superstition, paganism, and commercialism that characterize the site.

Second, since these healings, if they occur, fall into the same category as those of Christian Science or the New Age Movement, we must raise the possibility that Satan might be at work, doing what he can to deceive by doing as much "good" as he can.

We know that Satan can appear in whatever form he is expected. If you are a Catholic, he will appear as Mary; if you are a Protestant, he will appear as Jesus; if you are a Hindu, he will appear as Krishna. To put it simply, either miracles are based on Christ and the Bible or else they originate with the world of the occult, with its deceptions and demons.

The Catholic Church itself recognizes the possibility of deception. We can do no better than to accept the counsel of Ignatius of Loyola, who, when consulted about a young man who claimed that the wounds of Christ miraculously appeared in his hands, said that these marks (the stigmata) "might just as well have been the work of the devil as the work of God."[10] Agreed.

There are, after all, only two "miracle workers" in the universe. And unless we follow the teaching of Scripture, we can be deceived by miracles that have come from the other side of the spirit world. Right doctrine and right motives are the minimum we must look for in accepting God's miracles.

NOTES

Portions of this chapter first appeared in *Seven Convincing Miracles: Understanding the Claims of Christ in Today's Culture,* by Erwin W. Lutzer (Chicago: Moody, 1999).

1. *Citizen,* December 1997.
2. Emanuel Swedenborg, quoted in John Ankerberg and John Weldon, *The Facts on Channeling* (Chattanooga: John Ankerberg Evangelistic Association, 1998), 8.
3. *Chicago Sun-Times,* 14 October 1998.
4. *Chicago Sun-Times,* 1 March 1999.
5. "Modern Miracles Have Strict Rules," *Time,* 10 April 1995, 74.
6. B. B. Warfield, *Counterfeit Miracles* (London: Banner of Truth, 1918), 108.
7. Ibid., 124.
8. Dan Wakefield, *Expect a Miracle* (San Francisco: Harper, 1995), 30–31.
9. Ibid., 20.
10. Ignatius Loyola, quoted in Warfield, *Counterfeit Miracles,* 85.

WHEN YOU JUDGE CONDUCT

Can We Agree on What Is Right and Wrong?

Christians differ on matters of conduct.

We must never forget that some things are always wrong: It is always wrong to break the Ten Commandments; it is always wrong to be conformed to the world; it is always wrong to permit unwholesome words to proceed out of our mouths; it is always wrong to grieve the Holy Spirit. It is always wrong to feed our sensual appetites. The list could go on.

On the other hand there are some things that are always right: It is always right to love one another; it is always right to set our affection on things above, not on the things of earth; it is always right to be filled with the Spirit. It is always right to be honest and to respect other people.

However, there are some matters that are difficult to classify categorically as right or wrong; sinful or not sinful. Some things are a matter of conscience. In Europe Christians routinely drink wine or other fermented drinks; they are surprised that many American Christians believe in total abstinence. Many of us argue that given the curse of alcoholism, it is better to not take a single drink. But others counter that anything—including food—can be misused. In biblical times Jesus took water and turned it into wine. So the disagreements continue.

There was a time when we heard from the pulpit that no Christian should ever attend the theater; yet today, for good or for ill, Christians do so routinely. There was a time when Christians never participated in Sunday sports, yet today we honor Christian athletes even if their schedules do not allow them to attend church during the playing season. The list of dos and don'ts varies from culture to culture, from era to era.

How do we resolve these differences?

I am well aware that by discussing these matters, I am walking through a minefield. The most distinctive characteristic of a minefield is that the mines are hidden. So I am taking the risk of stepping on one unexpectedly, but we have to remember that one man's minefield is another's protection. So let's walk through this chapter together.

All of us are tempted to universalize our own personal convictions; we want to absolutize that which should be relative. We think that because we have a certain kind of music and worship style, everyone should do it our way. We would be shocked at how differently the people worship in other parts of the world; some are restricted and others worship with freedom in singing and dance. We are locked into our own culture much more than we realize. Yet we always want to absolutize our personal preferences.

The other temptation is to relativize sin. There is a tendency to make sin acceptable by reducing absolutes to cultural norms and perspectives. When we do that, we lower the standards, rather than rooting them in sound biblical principles. We should always be trying to find the balance between the dangers of legalism and the dangers of license.

> AT ROOT, LEGALISM IS A MATTER OF HEART AND MOTIVE.

A third problem is that we tend to define spirituality in terms of what we don't do. We like lists of dos and don'ts because they help us define the content of Christian living. Some of us remember the oft-used lingo "Don't drink, dance or chew, or go around with girls who do!" Some people still think that proof of conversion is to simply accept the right "rules."

Are those who keep rules—even strict rules—legalistic? Perhaps, and perhaps not. Legalism is the wrong use of laws or rules. If I keep the rules thinking that this makes me godly, then, yes, I am legalistic. Rules can keep me from certain select sins; what rules cannot do is give me righteousness. Rules do not cause me to love God or to strive for holiness. Jesus tried to get the Pharisees to see that rules cannot get to the heart.

Here in Chicago there is a section of the city with 160,000 inhabitants. None drinks a drop of liquor; not a one smokes; not a one dances; not a one goes to movies. I mentioned that to a friend, and he said that he would really like to visit this section of the city, maybe even move there. I told him that someday that might actually be possible. The area of the city, however, is Rose Hill Cemetery! You see, some who define the Christian life by what they *don't* do just miss the point.

But rules—even the negative ones—do have some value. They keep us from certain select sins. I'm glad for rules that kept me from certain sins during my youth, and we raised our children with many of the same standards. There are many things that are not wise to do; other things are downright wrong. There is value in the "Thou Shalt Nots," as the Ten Commandments remind us.

So let us not be critical of those who would keep rules; they might be legalistic, but not necessarily. Jesus did not mind the Pharisees' keeping their rules (though some of them went beyond the bounds of Scripture), but He grieved over the fact that they stopped short of developing intimacy with God.

To some people, this chapter will appear to deal with trivial matters. But when you are a member of the family of God and you want to please the Lord, even trivial sins are important. We have to please the Lord and work with one another, and that is no small task. Thus, we turn to the Bible to discuss the dos and don'ts, and hope that we can agree on the principles, if not the specific conduct. Two people can keep the same rules; one can do so legalistically because he believes that the rules define his relationship with God. Another can keep the same rules, but do so knowing that the important thing is to cultivate his relationship with God. At root, legalism is a matter of heart and motive.

DOS AND DON'TS

In first-century Rome, some of the converts to Christianity had a Jewish heritage, whereas others were converted out of paganism. Some of the converts were convinced that the dietary laws of the Old Testament should be kept; others accepted the new revelation that such requirements were a thing of the past. Paul wrote to give them principles and clarifications that are relevant for us today. He said that at times there can be two legitimate viewpoints and that we must accept one another and get along.

Don't Judge One Another

"Accept him whose faith is weak, without passing judgment on disputable matters. One man's faith allows him to eat everything, but another man, whose faith is weak, eats only vegetables" (Romans 14:1–2). How is this to be resolved? Paul continued, "The man who eats everything must not look down on him who does not, and the man who does not eat everything must not condemn the man who does, for God has accepted him" (v. 3). Those who understood God's new revelation of freedom from dietary laws (that is, those who were strong) should not judge those who did not feel free to eat meat (those who were weak).

Those who had freedom in this matter were regarded by Paul as the strong; those who felt they had to obey the ancient rules were the weak. If we had been there, we might have seen this quite differently. We probably would have said that the person who adhered to the old Jewish standards was the strong person and that the one who had freedom to eat anything was the weak Christian. We tacitly assume that the Christian who has the liberty to enjoy certain activities is the weak one, whereas the strong one is the person who believes that such freedom is capitulation to the world.

Paul said that the opposite was true. A strong Christian will see that morally neutral activities should not be categorically forbidden. A weak Christian will multiply taboos, still thinking that spiritual living is conforming to the right set of 'don'ts.' In Rome, the strong Christians could eat meat with a clear conscience; the weak Christians could not.

Paul's point was that neither the weak nor the strong should judge the other. If a person considers himself strong, he will not judge someone who is weak. The person who goes to the theater should not judge the one who refuses to go; but the one who refuses to go should not judge the one who goes —unless of course, we are talking about a risqué movie that no Christian should see.

> THERE IS ROOM FOR DIFFERENCES IN THE HOUSEHOLD OF GOD.

The point is that the theater itself is neutral; therefore, there has to be latitude without judging. The strong brother sees that the theater in itself is nothing, but he should not judge the weaker brother, who believes his presence there would be a compromise with the world.

Let us suppose that you, along with a number of others, were a servant in a household. Would it be your responsibility to judge the performance of one of your peers? No. Paul wrote, "Who are you to judge someone else's servant? To his own master he stands or falls. And he will stand, for the Lord is able to make him stand" (Romans 14:4). Then Paul went on to illustrate his point with the Sabbath. After the Jews were saved, they could not break the habit of observing the seventh day of the week rather than the first day (Sunday). What was Paul's response? He continued, "One man considers one day more sacred than another; another man considers every day alike. Each one should be fully convinced in his own mind" (v. 5).

Can you attend a football game on Sunday? If we say, well, it is fine to watch football on television, but we should not attend a game on Sunday, then we will be caught in a host of hair-splitting distinctions. The question actually is one of individual conscience, and we must not judge others regarding the matter. Our Master might permit one of His children to participate and not another. Before your own Master you stand or fall.

Should we not be concerned about how Sunday is being devalued because of sports, shopping, and traveling? Yes, we should be concerned, for although we worship God each day, Sunday is a special time when we gather with the people of God. But the answer is not to make a rule that fits every Christian! The answer is to teach people to love God more than they love sports. And to love the people of God more than they love shopping, or whatever.

Paul would say, whichever day we choose, whether Saturday or Sunday, as our special day; and whatever diet we adopt, we must worship and eat for the glory of God. If that is our motivation, then let us not judge each other. There is room for differences in the household of God.

Don't Cause a Brother or Sister to Stumble

"Therefore let us stop passing judgment on one another. Instead, make up your mind not to put any stumbling block or obstacle in your brother's way" (Romans 14:13). Paul repeats this point even more clearly a few verses later: "Do not destroy the work of God for the sake of food. All food is clean, but it is wrong for a man to eat anything that causes someone else to stumble. It is better not to eat meat or drink wine or to do anything else that will cause your brother to fall" (vv. 20–21).

What does it mean to put a stumbling block in your brother's way?

Let us consider a slightly different controversy that Paul confronted in the church in Corinth. This was a center of pagan worship and sexual permissiveness. Part of the pagan worship included eating meat offered to the gods. The priest would take the meat brought by the worshipers and put it on the altar. Later, this meat was taken to the marketplace and sold for less than a comparable cut that had come directly from the slaughterhouse.

> SO, WHAT DOES IT MEAN TO BECOME A STUMBLING BLOCK?

When the pagans became Christians, they realized that idols were nothing, so this meat was not polluted in any way. But there were some Christians who were weak in the faith. They remembered having worshiped those pagan gods, and they felt that if they ate meat which had been offered to those deities this would entangle them in their past idolatry. For them to eat the meat offered to idols would be to defile themselves.

You can imagine the disagreements.

"I can't believe that you would eat meat that was offered to Zeus."

"Wait now . . . who is Zeus? He is nothing, just an idol of stone."

"Yes, but behind those idols are demons."

"Yes, I grant that, but because I am a follower of Jesus, He takes what belonged to the pagan gods and sanctifies it."

One Christian accused the other of lack of separation from the world; the other would say that such an accusation was nothing but narrow-mindedness. Paul said that Christians have liberty on this issue, but that does not necessarily mean that Christians should exercise that liberty even if they have knowledge (that is, the understanding that an idol is nothing). Simply because some believers knew they could eat meat that did not mean that they *should* eat meat. Admittedly, God had declared all foods clean, but because some Christians believed that eating was a concession to paganism, he wrote, "Be careful, however, that the exercise of your freedom does not become a stumbling block to the weak" (1 Corinthians 8:9).

So, what does it mean to become a stumbling block? This does not mean that we should never do anything that another Christian doesn't like! Christ frequently said and did things that caused offense—even to His own disciples. If He had been concerned about offending the Pharisees, He would not have healed people on the Sabbath, nor would He have eaten with publicans and sinners. These actions raised the ire of the religious cliques beyond measure, but He did them anyway.

For Paul, being a stumbling block meant to do something that would make a brother or sister fall back into his or her former way of life of sin. Imagine that the weaker brother is invited to the home of a stronger brother, who serves meat. The weaker brother asks whether this has been offered to idols, and the stronger brother says, "Yes, it was." Now the weaker one believes he is being drawn back to his former associations with pagan gods. The one brother has put the other brother in a predicament where he must either be impolite or violate his conscience. Paul says, "Don't do that."

Although the following sounds like a trivial illustration, I tell it because I was a personal witness to it. One man, who spent all of his spare time gambling and drinking in a pool hall, was soundly converted. Months later he was invited into the home of a Christian couple who had a pool table in their basement. The new Christian gasped when he saw the table; he could not believe that Christians would play that game, which in his mind was so sinful. The older Christian man was surprised at the reaction of his new friend. What could possibly be wrong with playing pool? The answer, of course, is nothing. But it would be sin for him to insist that the new Christian play the game. In fact, it would be better to not play the game at all than to force his brother to compromise his convictions.

If drinking wine tempts my brother to return to alcoholism; if inviting him to a football game revives in him the obsession he once had for sports; if attending a theater leads him back to his life of sensual pleasure, then I should not do these things, even if I have freedom to do so. "Therefore, if what I eat causes my brother to fall into sin, I will never eat meat again, so that I will not cause him to fall" (1 Corinthians 8:13).

We are not only responsible for ourselves but for one another.

Don't Violate Your Conscience

Paul continues his instructions to the church at Rome. "So whatever you believe about these things keep between

yourself and God. Blessed is the man who does not condemn himself by what he approves. But the man who has
doubts is condemned if he eats, be-
cause his eating is not from faith;
and everything that does not come
from faith is sin" (Romans 14:22–
23). This principle applies equally
to the weak and the strong. The
weak brother should not do anything that he cannot do in faith,
even if it is a harmless activity. Nor should the strong brother do something that he does not believe is right and good
for him. If it violates your conscience, *don't do it.*

> GOD DOES NOT EX-
> IST FOR US; WE EXIST
> FOR GOD. IT'S ALL
> ABOUT HIM AND
> NOT ABOUT US.

Since the conscience is tempered by environment, some
people might feel convicted doing the most trivial things. In
time they may begin to accept God's revelation regarding
Christian liberty on a particular point. Until that happens,
such are sinning if they can't do these things with a clear
conscience. And the strong brother should not have a clear
conscience if he is causing another believer to stumble.

Today there are certain card games that have their origin
in occultism. I personally don't play any card games, and I
for one would not want to play such games with occult
symbols or associations. That is my deep conviction, so if I
played, I would violate my conscience. However, when I
walked into a Christian retirement center, I noticed that
many of the people were playing these games. My first reaction was to judge them and say that no Christian should
play these games, and that furthermore, they are a waste of
time. Think of what could be done if each retiree were to

take an interest in missionaries, write them letters, and pray for their children!

Yet upon further thought, I must allow for individual conscience. Just as meat offered to idols was sanctified by the Word of God and prayer, so card games in the hands of Christians might be nothing more than that—cards with pictures. Paul might say, "You, then, why do you judge your brother? Or why do you look down on your brother? For we will all stand before God's judgment seat. . . . So then, each of us will give an account of himself to God" (Romans 14:10, 12).

Yes, as we have learned, there are times when we must judge, but let us be sure to judge ourselves first. And let us make sure that we do not violate our consciences.

Don't Serve Self, but God

In the next chapter, Paul gives the fourth principle we must follow. "May the God who gives endurance and encouragement give you a spirit of unity among yourselves as you follow Christ Jesus, so that with one heart and mouth you may glorify the God and Father of our Lord Jesus Christ. Accept one another, then, just as Christ accepted you, in order to bring praise to God" (Romans 15:5–7).

To live a life that glorifies God means that we transcend the rules; such a motivation transcends the legalist who wants the Christian life reduced to a series of dos and don'ts. It transcends the self-righteous Christian whose freedom has led to license. Here is a principle that exposes our hearts and becomes the basis for all conduct.

You tell me that you have the freedom to attend a theater? If you do, make sure that you attend only those movies that will help you to glorify God. You have the freedom to watch television? You had best watch only those programs that will help you glorify God. And all of us must be prepared to shut off the television when the programs we watch no longer help us to glorify the One we love and serve. God does not exist for us; we exist for God. It's all about Him and not about us.

If you tell me that you have the freedom to drink wine, you make sure to do it to the glory of God; let it not lead to drunkenness. If you tell me that you have the freedom to play professional sports on Sunday, you had best do it to the glory of God and have the willpower to change your vocation if it interferes with pleasing the One who redeemed you. You say that you have the freedom to dance; do it for the glory of God and be prepared to quit when you can no longer do so.

> A CHRISTIAN IS MUCH MORE THAN A SINNER MINUS HIS SINS.

You have the freedom to use the Internet? Use it to glorify God and switch it off before you begin to look at material that no longer glorifies God. It is the Lord we serve.

Consider our example: "We who are strong ought to bear with the failings of the weak and not to please ourselves. Each of us should please his neighbor for his good, to build him up. For even Christ did not please himself but, as it is written: 'The insults of those who insult you have fallen on me'" (Romans 15:1–3).

For even Christ did not please Himself!

Clearly, when we live by this standard, we learn that Christianity is not a matter of rules but *relationship*. The dos and don'ts are only the first steps in learning that some things are wrong. The closer we live to the Lord, the more we realize that even neutral activities become sin when they occupy time and energy that could be used for eternal values. Once we grasp this concept, we will be more and more hesitant to judge others, because we see our own failures and sins more clearly.

Finally, if we lived by this principle, we would see the total impossibility of living the Christian life! God's desire for purity would loom so large that we would be driven to Him for supernatural ability. Petty distinctions would pale in comparison to the weightier matters of honesty, a deep affection for God, and the fruit of the Spirit. We would feel helpless, morally weak, and inadequate. We would have a new perspective that would make dependence on God a necessity for living the Christian life.

Christ has not trapped us into being good while others can have a good time! His restrictions were given to us to show us more keenly our need of Him; but it is our relationship with Him that matters. A Christian is much more than a sinner minus his sins. No wonder Christ said that He came to give us life and to give it more abundantly.

If you and I were arrested for being Christians, would there be enough evidence to convict us? That is the first prerequisite for genuine Christian conduct!

11

WHEN YOU JUDGE CHARACTER

What Are the Marks of Integrity?

Y ou might remember the name Richard Dortch, who was the associate of Jim Bakker during the famous scandal of the mid-eighties. Dortch, who tried to set up hush money for Jessica Hahn, the woman with whom Bakker had a relationship, eventually went to prison. Dortch was a good man who made an unwise decision under the pressure of trying to save a ministry. Later he wrote a book called *Integrity: How I Lost It and My Journey Back.*[1]

Integrity is sometimes better described than defined. There are many uses of the word in Scripture. For example, God called Job a man of integrity. After Job's children died, we read that God said to Satan, "Have you considered my servant Job? There is no one on earth like him; he is blameless and upright, a man who fears God and shuns evil. And he still maintains his integrity, though you incited me

against him to ruin him without any reason" (2:3). Jesus
was recognized as one who had integrity. When the Pharisees sent their disciples to trap Jesus, they began by saying,
"Teacher, we know that you are a man of integrity" (Matthew
22:16).

But integrity is in short supply: Some 70 percent of college students say that they cheat—if you can believe they
told the truth to the pollster![2] We are full of fine talk about
how desperately our society needs integrity, but somehow it
is always something that *others* should have.

We want our politicians to have it.

We want our children to have it.

We want our corporations to have it.

We want our schools to have it.

We want our church leaders to have it.

Stephen Carter, in his book *Integrity,* maintains that it is
perhaps "first among virtues because . . . in some sense [it]
is prior to everything else: the rest of what we think matters
very little if we lack essential integrity, and the courage of
our convictions, the willingness to act and speak on behalf
of what is right."[3]

Carter defines integrity as something very specific and
requiring three steps: (a) *discerning* what is right and wrong;
(b) *acting* on what you have discerned, even at personal
cost; and (c) *saying openly* that you are acting on your understanding of right from wrong.[4] In other words, a person
of integrity should not be ashamed that he or she is living
this way. This is often difficult because of our natural desire
to conform. But the more public we are about our commitment to integrity, the more motivated we will be to live by
our standards.

The word *integrity* comes from the same Latin root as *integer*, a "whole number." So the word carries the meaning of wholeness; we are people of integrity when we are whole persons, as whole numbers that are not divided. And this includes the idea of "the serenity of a person who is confident in the knowledge that he or she is living rightly."[5] Warren Wiersbe quips, "God wants to make integers; Satan wants to make fractions."[6]

> WE ARE CALLED UPON TO DRAW A STRAIGHT FURROW IN A CROOKED WORLD.

There is a difference between one's character (integrity) and one's reputation. D. L. Moody said that character was what a man was in the dark. Unfortunately, our generation finds it difficult to distinguish character from reputation; only one's reputation seems to matter in our careless generation. But actually our character is more important than our reputation. People can damage your reputation, but they cannot damage your character. We read in Proverbs, "The integrity of the upright guides them, but the unfaithful are destroyed by their duplicity" (11:3).

INTEGRITY AND THE EVANGELICAL COMMUNITY

Charles Colson is quite right when he reminds us that many people will make up their minds about the gospel based on our lifestyle. We've all met people who tell us that they were "turned off" by the church because of a lack of integrity, or hypocritical self-righteousness. We do not have to look back to the high-profile scandals of the 1980s to witness the loss of integrity within the believing church.

Here are some examples of how we lose our integrity:

- When a Christian organization raises funds for one project but uses the funds for another.
- When a fund-raising letter exaggerates a story so that we will become angry (conventional wisdom says that only angry people send money!) and also exaggerates the ability of the organization to deal with the problem. Just think of the number of letters you have received that give the impression if we send our money to _____ we will be able to successfully fight abortionists, pornographers, the ACLU, and so on. There might be some value in supporting these organizations, but if their claims were true, we would be more successful in stopping the impact of the targeted groups.
- When Christian publishers are more driven by sales than the value (integrity) of their products.
- When ministers, evangelists, and leaders overexaggerate the size of their meetings, the number of their converts, and the benefits of their ministry.
- When churches are more concerned about numerical growth than the possible compromises by which that growth has been achieved.
- When pastors constantly preach about the positive aspects of the Christian faith but never instruct their people about God's wrath, hell, and repentance.
- When a Bible translation changes the meaning of Scripture to accommodate the spirit of the age.
- When we tolerate open sin among church members and refuse to discipline them.

- When we see abuses, false teachers, and breaches of integrity but remain silent for fear of "getting involved" or of being unpopular.

If it is true that God honors integrity, we should strive toward this virtue even at great personal cost. If Christians are not known for integrity, it is doubtful that we will be known for much else. Integrity lies at the heart of strong families; it is the foundation of effective ministries and our witness to the world. We are called upon to draw a straight furrow in a crooked world.

Yet, for all of the faults of the church, it is still better to be a part of a local body of believers than to cut ourselves off from fellowship and go it alone. The church is, after all, God's only plan for representing the gospel in the world. To quote Warren Wiersbe again, "I'd rather be a struggling Christian in an imperfect church than a perfect sinner outside the church."[7]

And yet, we must ask: If we act with truthfulness and wholeness, what standard shall we use? Many people have integrity but only as defined by their own warped standards, or according to their inactive consciences. Thoreau was right when he said that someone's willingness to die for a cause does not make that cause right. Lest we measure ourselves by ourselves, we need to find a more objective yardstick by which integrity can be judged.

Psalm 15:1 asks a question. "LORD, who may dwell in your sanctuary? Who may live on your holy hill?" Then follows the description of the man whom God receives, the one who is allowed to scale the hill of the Lord and be pleasing to Him.

These characteristics are easy to practice among those

who share our views of integrity but very difficult to practice in the business world. Honesty comes easy if you work with honest people who are blessed with the grace of integrity. But I have a friend who works as a manager in a car dealership, surrounded by cheating, chiseling, and lying. Every day he must face the question: *To what extent am I willing to let my integrity show? What price am I willing to pay, either from those who supervise me or from those whom I supervise?* Integrity is difficult in a world where it is in scarce supply. Integrity costs.

CHARACTERISTICS OF INTEGRITY

We can do no better than to walk though Psalm 15, stopping long enough to identify and contemplate the lifestyle of the person who has the kind of integrity that pleases God.

He Speaks the Truth

"He whose walk is blameless and who does what is righteous, who speaks truth from his heart and has no slander on his tongue" (Psalm 15:2–3). Under what conditions does he speak the truth? He speaks the truth even if it costs him.

He speaks the truth when it diminishes him. Perhaps he has to admit to a sinful past; or maybe he has to tell the truth about what happened at work. He speaks the truth even if it puts other people in a better light. He speaks the truth when he must make a confession to his wife.

He speaks the truth when doing so shames him. Recently I heard about a Christian leader who, when confronted with the accusation of having an affair on the Internet, denied it —until the evidence was presented to him. Our penchant to hide sin is so powerful that it is almost impossible to tell the truth about ourselves *to* ourselves, much less to others!

The person of integrity speaks the truth when it harms him. Many years ago here in Chicago a baseball manager lost a game because he pointed out that his home run hitter did not touch third base. The player was livid because the ump hadn't noticed the infraction; but for this manager, truth was truth. Honesty was honesty.

He speaks the truth when it indicts him. I know of a man who claimed injuries on the job when actually he was injured in a hunting accident. He will be getting workman's compensation for the rest of his life. When a visiting minister told this man that he had to confess to the compensation board, he responded, "Do you think I want to be in jail?"

But there are some things worse than jail: one is to be out of fellowship with the living God because of some sin we have not been willing to make right. A man of integrity would rather go to jail than to have sin on his conscience that cuts him off from the blessing of God.

We all ought to pray, "Save me, O LORD, from lying lips and from deceitful tongues" (Psalm 120:2). And our lost integrity can be restored if we remember, "He who conceals his sins does not prosper, but whoever confesses and renounces them finds mercy" (Proverbs 28:13).

He Honors Friendships

The man of integrity is the one who "has no slander on his tongue, who does his neighbor no wrong and casts no slur on his fellowman" (Psalm 15:3). Someone has said, "If you want to find out who your friends are, just make one big, public mistake." Some of your friends will quickly run for cover, denying any close relationship. But your true friends will stand by you. To the man of integrity, his friend's reputation will be much more important than his own. Blessed are those who honor friendships.

Here is a scenario that happens so often that you can be sure a story like this is happening even as you read this book. A person is relieved of his responsibility within an organization; maybe he is dismissed from the church staff or from serving on the board of a parachurch ministry. Perhaps he was asked to leave because of incompetence, perhaps dishonesty, or moral questions. Or maybe he does not have the right gift mix, and therefore he was not the best fit for the job.

PEOPLE OF INTEGRITY DO NOT MAKE THEMSELVES LOOK BETTER THAN THEY ARE.

Only the pastor or his manager knows all the reasons for the dismissal, but whoever dismissed him must remain silent. He does not want to damage the person's reputation; he does not want to hurt his family or jeopardize the man's future. The leader, hopefully, is a person of integrity so he can be trusted to keep the sordid details to himself.

The fired employee knows he can depend on the pastor/employer not to "tell the whole truth" about why he was dismissed. So now he is free to give any reason he wants as to why he was fired; he can stir up sympathy and do as much damage as he can for the leader, who is left to put the pieces back together. In fact, the dismissed employee might not even tell his wife the whole story of why he was asked to leave. He is free to tell part of the truth, to shade the truth, or to make up the "truth" as he wills. He can make himself look as good as he wishes while he makes the manager look bad. There is not much that can be done about it.

If the leader has integrity, he will simply take the slander and not try to justify himself; he will simply accept this burden of leadership and manage the criticism as best he can. If the dismissed employee had integrity, he would have spoken well of the decision, whether he agreed with it or not. He also could have encouraged others to continue their support of the ministry. In short, he could have put the best face on it, knowing that God uses even injustices to hone us. Someone has wisely said, "Your friends can only take you up to your potential; only your enemies can take you beyond it." At any rate, people of integrity do not make themselves look better than they are.

Integrity!

He Keeps Commitments

David continues the description of the man of integrity who "despises a vile man but honors those who fear the LORD, who keeps his oath even when it hurts" (Psalm 15:4). *He keeps his oath even when it hurts!*

We think immediately of the oath of marriage. The vow does not say, "I will love you as long as you provide the satisfaction I deserve." Or, "I will love you until I find someone who is more compatible with my personality." However tragically necessary a divorce might be, the fact is that we cannot preside over the death of a marriage without grieving.

We must mourn the loss of integrity when, for whatever reason, the vows so solemnly taken are later broken.

A promise is more than just a sentence spoken with words. A promise is a statement about how one intends to live and what one intends to do. Admittedly, promises sometimes have implied conditions. "I will meet you for breakfast" means that I will be there, all things being equal. We would not say that it is a breach of integrity if you could not make the appointment for any number of valid reasons. But those who lack integrity will use any excuse to avoid a commitment. Indeed, some make a commitment of one kind or another knowing that they cannot or will not keep their promise.

Can you trust people to keep a secret? For the most part, you can, if it does not affect their own egos. But people—even those you thought had integrity—will not, for the most part, keep their promise if they can benefit themselves by telling it. They will break their word if the story will bolster their "self-esteem." Or if they are falsely accused and telling the secret will make themselves look good, don't expect them to keep their word. Our desire to protect ourselves is so strong that we will make exceptions whenever it suits us.

Alternatively, people will sometimes keep silent, even betraying friends, if speaking up costs them something. A young pastor, a friend of mine, was asked by the elders in his first church to visit a wealthy farmer who had a great influence in the community. He attended the church occasionally and supported it financially. Specifically, the elders requested that the young pastor ask the man whether he was saved. "We are not sure where he stands spiritually," they said.

The pastor visited the man and, perhaps naively, asked him, "Are you saved?" The man was livid and told the pastor that he was insulted. The offended man attended the next business meeting, stood up and said, "This pastor had the nerve to ask me whether I was a Christian. What do you think we should do about it?" Then he sat down.

Dead silence.

The man rose again, "I think we should ask him to leave." A vote was taken and the pastor was dismissed—and not one elder stood to defend him! Only the janitor who heard the meeting over the downstairs speaker put his arm around him and told him he was sorry for what had happened. The pastor left the church and walked several miles in the rain, disbelieving what had just happened. Not surprisingly, he never pastored again. Not one elder—the *wimps!*—stood to defend him or explain that he had visited the man at their direction!

Where is integrity?

He Refuses to Take Advantage of Others

The man of integrity is one who "lends his money without usury and does not accept a bribe against the innocent" (Psalm 15:5). We should not interpret this to mean that he might accept a bribe against someone who is not innocent. No, the text simply means that he is the kind of person who will not take advantage of others. He will not up his price just because he thinks he can get away with it.

The Old Testament rule that usury (we call it interest) should not be exacted has nothing to do with our modern custom of receiving interest for our investments. If I am lending you money that will help you make money, I have a right to get a return on my investment. The point God was making is that it was unfair to receive usury from the poor, who have no chance of making money with money. We are not to take advantage of one another.

Integrity can still be found if we look far enough. A Christian man encouraged missionaries and Christian workers to buy a certain mining stock, because there was hard evidence it would go up in price. Indeed it did. But when the mine collapsed, so did the stock, and many fine people lost their money.

What did this man do? Legally, he had no obligation to do anything. Everyone knows that when you invest in the stock market there is the possibility of losing the money. But this man—bless him—liquidated all of his assets and paid everyone what they had put into the market. Here is a man who could neither be bought nor sold; a man who went beyond the call of duty in the interest of being godly, rather than being driven by self-interest. Contrast this with the famous Enron scandal that took place in the year 2002, and we can soon see that such integrity is rare indeed.

He Is Not for Sale

The experts tell us that everyone is for sale. Wave big money before them, and they will throw away their integrity if the price is right. This is why we are admonished, "Buy the truth and do not sell it; get wisdom, discipline and understanding" (Proverbs 23:23).

Are you for sale?

There is a story about a man who said to a woman, "Would you sleep with me for $50,000?" She thought for a minute and said, "For $50, 000 . . . yes, I think I would." He then said, "Would you do it for $50?" to which she indignantly replied, "What do think I am?" He answered, "We already know what you are; now we're only dickering about the price."

Let it be said that we are not for sale. Some things are worth being fired for; some things are worth losing your inheritance for; some things are worth going to jail for; some things are worth failing in college for. Blessed are those who have the truth and will not sell it for a price.

The English statesman and writer Thomas More was a Catholic, so it goes without saying that I disagree with his theology. But I do admire his integrity. Remember when King Henry VIII insisted that More sign on to the Act of Supremacy that made King Henry the head of the English Church? Thomas More, however, staunch Catholic that he was, would not have Henry supersede the authority of the Pope. He said no to his longtime friend even though he knew it could cost him his life. And it did.

The popular adage "Well, a man has to live" is simply not true. The martyrs throughout the history of the church would tell us that there are some things worth dying for. Blessed are they who do not love their lives more than they love the gospel. Blessed are those who believe that integrity is more important than whatever the world might have to replace it. Such a person can ascend to God's Holy Hill; He pleases the Lord.

INTEGRITY'S BOTTOM LINE

There are many lessons we must learn about integrity.

First, it is fragile. Once you have lost it, it takes much time to get it back—if ever. It is not like spilling a bucket of water and then returning to fill it again. A better illustration is that integrity is like a vase on a mantel that drops to the floor and needs to be glued back. And even after you have glued it, some hairline cracks still show where the break was.

If you don't believe that integrity is fragile, try doing business with a friend you have defrauded. Or try to reestablish a relationship with your wife to whom you have lied. I gave some information to a friend, and he promised to keep it secret. But he passed it on to the very people I did not want to know. Now, if we have lunch together I only tell him things I want other people to know. Barclay quotes someone as saying, "There are three things which come not back—the spent arrow, the spoken word, and the lost opportunity."[8]

Second, losing your integrity begins with small infractions. Years before a tire blows, hairline cracks develop that widen under pressure. What you see when the vehicle goes off the road was long in the making. Just so, hidden character flaws might take years to become noticeable. The man whom you catch in dishonesty has probably been dishonest for a long time.

To the yet-to-be-married reading this, let me give a word of advice. If you are dating a man and you find him to be dishonest, be assured that you are not the first person to whom he has lied and also be assured that you will not be the last person to whom he will lie. Breaches of integrity might appear as isolated occurrences, but usually they are symptomatic of a pattern of behavior.

Third, restoring integrity begins with repentance. We've all had lapses in integrity; when we do fall short, integrity can only be restored through a thorough and honest examination of our hearts. Then we must be willing to do anything to be fully right with God and man. We are never more like the devil than when we lie.

> WE MUST BE
> PEOPLE OF
> DISCERNMENT,
> NO MATTER
> THE COST.

To someone who struggles with lying, I give this sure cure to be delivered from this sin: The moment you are dishonest, confess it immediately to the person affected. Stop a conversation in mid-sentence and say, "What I just told you was a lie." This, I believe, will be one way to train your heart and mind in the discipline of truth-telling.

The historian Josephus tells a famous story of ten thousand Jews who, when the Roman General Petronius was ordered to erect a statue of the Emperor Caligula in the temple in Jerusalem, protested, baring their throats and insisting that they would rather die than become idolaters. After the negotiations, Petronius was sufficiently moved by their courage and wrote the emperor saying that his honor would not allow him to place the statue in the temple.[9] Those who would rather die than compromise their religious beliefs are indeed examples of integrity, whether we agree with their beliefs or not.

If we expect to have a lasting impact on the world; if we expect God to bless our efforts in sharing the gospel and being "salt and light," we must know how to distinguish the church from the world. We must be people of discernment, no matter the cost. At the root of these judgments lies integrity, that quality of character that stands against the selfism that permeates our culture. Perhaps we can do no better than to quote the words of Job, "Let me be weighed in a just balance and let God know my integrity!" (Job 36:1 NRSV).

Let us call on God, asking Him to give us both the desire and the ability to be people of truth in our decaying society. And, by His grace, let us be the church, that body whose impact is greater than its numbers; that body that has a message by which we can be transformed.

> Rise up, O church of God!
> Have done with lesser things;
> Give heart and soul and mind and strength
> To serve the King of kings.
>
> Lift high the cross of Christ!
> Tread where His feet have trod;
> As brothers of the Son of Man
> Rise up, O church of God!

Notes

1. Richard W. Dortch, *Integrity: How I Lost It and My Journey Back* (Green Forest, Ark.: New Leaf, 1993).
2. Stephen Carter, *Integrity* (1996; New York: HarperTrade, 1997; New York: Basic Books, HarperCollins, 1996), 4.
3. Ibid., 7.
4. Ibid.
5. Ibid.
6. Warren W. Wiersbe, *The Integrity Crisis* (Nashville: Thomas Nelson, 1988), 20.
7. Ibid., 11.

8. William Barclay, *The Letter to the Romans* (Edinburgh: St. Andrew: 1965), 179.

9. Carter, *Integrity*, 15.

Great titles by Erwin Lutzer from Moody Press

CRIES FROM THE CROSS

To stand at the foot of the cross is to witness the purpose for which God created the world.

Before the cross we can only stand with bowed heads and a broken spirit. It is there that we see the attributes of God on display; and if we look carefully, we will see ourselves.

"The crucifixion of Jesus Christ brings us face to face with two seemingly contrary attributes of God—His love and His wrath, with two seemingly contradictory doctrines—the sovereignty of God and the free will of man. Once we understand Calvary, we can understand what it is to deny ourselves, take up our cross daily and follow Him. This is a work we should all read."

Kay Arthur, Precept Ministries

"With his unique insights and careful devotion to the text, Erwin Lutzer takes us deep into the mysteries of the Incarnation, no more powerfully revealed than in our Lord's seven statements from the cross. This is not just compelling reading, this is divinely profound truth."

John MacArthur, Grace Community Church

ISBN: 0-8024-0942-3
Hardback

MOODY
The Name You Can Trust
1-800-678-8812 www.MoodyPress.org

ISBN: 0-8024-2719-7

How You Can Be Sure That You Will Spend Eternity With God

It is possible to know, in this life, where you will spend eternity? In this concise and powerful book Erwin Lutzer explains why you can know, even now, where you will be after death. He insists that many who expect to enter heaven will discover that they were sadly mistaken. But it is not too late for those who are still living to choose the right path—and know it! No matter how much you know about the Gospel, this compelling book will provide a radical understanding of God's grace and power. This book is for you! And for a friend!

Your Eternal Reward

In this provocative book, Dr. Erwin Lutzer gives good reasons why there will be tears in heaven. When we reflect on how we lived for Christ, we might weep on the other side of the celestial gates. This book challenges widespread misconceptions about the judgment seat of Christ that have emptied it of its meaning. Although Christians have been justified by faith, Christ will still judge them for the "deeds done in the body.whether good or bad" (2 Corinthians 5:10). How well or poorly we do here might indeed determine our status in heaven for all eternity. No one who reads this book will ever see the experiences of life in quite the same way again.

ISBN: 0-8024-4192-0

One Minute After You Die

One minute after you slip behind the parted curtain, you will either be enjoying a personal welcome from Christ or catching your first glimpse of gloom as you have never known it. Either way, your future will be irrevocably fixed and eternally unchangeable. Lutzer urges us to study what the Bible has to say so we might comfort believers and warn unbelievers about the eternity that waits them.

ISBN: 0-8024-6322-3

MOODY
The Name You Can Trust
1-800-678-8812 www.MoodyPress.org